30 Old Testament QuickSkits For Kids

STEVEN JAMES

Standard®
PUBLISHING

Cincinnati, Ohio

DEDICATION

To Sonya Haskins—wife, mother, friend, and survivor.

THANKS & ACKNOWLEDGMENTS

To Dana and Liesl, for their research, typing, and time; to my daughters, Trinity and Ariel, for their ideas and suggestions; to Ruth Frederick, Christina Wallace, and Pamela Harty for their encouragement, guidance, flexibility, and motivation to help me see this project through to completion; to Mr. Thurmond's 3rd grade class and Mr. Collins' 9th grade class at Providence Academy, for helping me test-drive these stories; to Mark Collins, Sonya Haskins, Pam Johnson, and Jeff Keeling for their keen insights and thoughtful suggestions.

Published by Standard Publishing, Cincinnati, Ohio
www.standardpub.com

15 14 13 12 11 10   5 6 7 8 9 10 11 12 13
ISBN-13: 978-0-7847-1629-8
ISBN-10: 0-7847-1629-3

Edited by Christine Spence and Christina Wallace
Cover design by Joel Armstrong
Cover illustrations by Paula Becker
Interior design by Dale Meyers

TABLE OF CONTENTS

How to Use This Book

QuickSkits (otherwise known as reader's theatre scripts) are super-easy to use and aren't intimidating for students because there aren't any lines to memorize.

Just choose your story, photocopy the scripts, hand them out to your students, and you have an instant lesson.

Each kid-friendly skit retells a Bible story in a fun and creative way using 3-9 students.

These stories are written for live presentation. They can be performed using actors and actresses, puppets, or a mixture of the two. You could even record students reading the parts for an old-fashioned radio show.

Here are some simple steps to help you make the most of this book.

Step #1: Read the script.

Before class, read through the complete QuickSkit and look for any words or concepts that your students might not understand. Pay special attention to unusual names that your students might not recognize or be unable to pronounce. Later, when you call the children forward to present the story, you can tell them how to pronounce the unusual names.

You may wish to glance through the Table of Contents, Scripture Verse Index, or the Topical Index to find just the right story for your group.

Step #2: Assign parts.

As you review the script, consider which of your students would best fit the different reading parts. Typically, the narrator (or narrators) of the story have the longest reading parts and should be more experienced at reading aloud. For all the parts, you'll want to choose children who are comfortable reading aloud and presenting in front of a group. Some parts are humorous and contain silly comments or jokes. Don't be afraid to choose kids who like to ham it up for those parts!

If you have younger children in your class, (or children who aren't comfortable reading in front of others), you could use adults or teen volunteers to read the scripts instead. The reading level is targeted for 3rd-4th grade and up.

Step #3: Research the story.

Look up the story in the Bible. Scripture references are included with each skit. Read it through to understand its context. The QuickSkits are based upon Bible stories, but have been adapted for live performance. Some stories are condensed or revised, and others include only selective parts of the story (so that it remains age-appropriate for children).

You'll want to familiarize yourself with the Bible story so that you can answer any questions that might arise after the QuickSkit has been presented.

Step #4: Photocopy the scripts.

If you have enough copies of this book to give one to each child, do that. Otherwise, you'll need to make enough copies of the QuickSkit to give one copy to each of the readers (photocopy permission is granted for this purpose). Make one extra copy for yourself so that you can follow along and help prompt a child if she can't find her part, or stumbles over the pronunciation of a word. You may wish to place each script in a black folder (or a different colored folder for each part) so that the audience doesn't see the scripts. It's a little touch, but it can add class to the performance.

Use a highlight marker to identify the speaking parts for each specific story character. This makes it much easier for children to locate their lines and follow along in their script.

Decide whether or not you wish to use any costumes or props for the story. If there are suggested props for the story, gather those at this time.

Step #5: Hand out the scripts.

Now that you've familiarized yourself with the story, identified any sections that might cause your students to stumble, and chosen which students to call forward, your before-class preparation is done. Your next step is to bring the students up and hand out the scripts. Depending upon the confidence you have in the reading ability of your students, you may wish to give them the scripts before class and let them practice before performing the story in front of the rest of the group.

Give them a moment to look over the scripts while you introduce the story. (Make sure your readers know that they're not supposed to read the italicized stage directions aloud.)

In most cases, it's not crucial whether you choose a boy or a girl for a specific reading part. Sometimes it might be funny to have a girl play a part that's obviously a boy's part (such as Samson), or a boy play a girl's part (such as Delilah). In any case, if you reverse gender roles be sure you mention that to the audience. Children won't always know just by the name if a Bible character is male or female and you don't want them to be confused or misinformed.

Use discretion about whether or not to choose girls for reading parts that involve Jesus or God the Father. There are specific theological reasons why Jesus was male (for example, he is the Groom and gave up his life for his bride, the Church—see Ephesians 5:25, Mark 2:19-20. And God was Jesus' Father, not his mother—Mary was).

Step #6: Sit back and enjoy!

Once you're ready to begin, go and sit toward the front of the class with the rest of the listeners. Say, "OK, let's give them a hand and get started! Lights . . . Camera . . . Action!"

Don't stay onstage with the students while they're performing because they'll naturally look to you for prompts and help if they get lost. If a director stands onstage, children often turn their backs to the audience, and face the director instead. Also, you can coach and direct your actors and actresses more easily from the front row of the audience.

When the QuickSkit is finished, lead the listeners in applauding for the readers to thank them for their hard work!

What do I need to tell the students about acting and performing?

Encourage the students to look up at the audience whenever possible during the story so that their eyes aren't on the scripts the whole time. At first they might not look up at all, but their eye contact will improve the more they practice performing QuickSkits and the more comfortable they become reading aloud.

Tell them, "Remember not to hold the script in front of your face; the audience will want to see you while you're reading! And never turn your back to the listeners. Remember, you're telling the story to them, not to the other people on stage."

Remind the students not to go on with their lines if the audience is busy laughing. Wait until the laughter dies down before continuing or no one will hear the words.

Sometimes, one student might be a little slow in finding his or her lines. When that happens, the other readers might say something like, "Hey! Narrator! Say your part!" Stop this if you see it happening. Instead, encourage your students not to interrupt or correct each other, but only to read their own lines and leave the prompting to you, the director.

As the children perform, you may wish to encourage them to act out certain parts of the story. For example, when Goliath gets killed you could say, "OK, Goliath, fall over dead!" For the most part though, encourage them only to act out those things that are specifically mentioned in the scripts. Otherwise, they might get confused or lose their place.

Can I change the scripts in this book?

Feel free to make minor editorial changes to the scripts in this book. You may wish to leave out a joke that wouldn't make sense to your listeners, or delete a phrase that might be misunderstood. (However, permission is not granted to alter the stories in such a way that you change the theological meaning or intent of the story.)

Do we need special costumes or props?

Unless otherwise noted, no special costumes are needed for the stories. However, you may wish to use some silly costumes for various characters or stories. Use general stage lighting and microphones (if your audience is large). Make sure the listeners can hear the performers and won't be distracted by other things going on in the room.

Why do we still tell Old Testament stories today?

Psalm 78:1-7 (NLT) explains that we share God's ancient stories so that this generation (and the ones to come) will turn to the Lord and place their faith in him:

O my people, listen to my teaching.
Open your ears to what I am saying,
for I will speak to you in a parable.

I will teach you hidden lessons from our past—
stories we have heard and know,
stories our ancestors handed down to us.

We will not hide these truths from our children
but will tell the next generation about the
glorious deeds of the Lord.
We will tell of his power and the mighty miracles
he did.

For he issued his decree to Jacob;
he gave his law to Israel.
He commanded our ancestors
to teach them to their children,

so the next generation might know them—
even the children not yet born—
that they in turn might teach their children.

So each generation can set its hope anew on God,
remembering his glorious miracles
and obeying his commands.

In addition, the stories of the Old Testament were written to teach us and give us hope: *"For everything that was written in the past was written to teach us, so that through endurance and the encouragement of the Scriptures we might have hope"* (Romans 15:4).

Finally, stories of the Israelites's struggles in the Old Testament serve as examples of moral choices and warnings about the consequences of sin. Why? *"To keep us from setting our hearts on evil things as they did. . . . These things happened to them as examples and were written down as warnings for us"* (1 Corinthians 10:6, 11).

So use these stories for instruction, encouragement, and warning.

Summary

As you present these stories, remember to encourage your students to face the audience and use plenty of facial expressions, sound effects, and natural gestures. Encourage them to respond to the audience, have fun, and enjoy themselves![*]

---

*For more extensive tips on creative storytelling and suggestions for using reader's theater, see my book **The Creative Storytelling Guide for Children's Ministry** (Standard Publishing, 2002). For scripts written specifically for two actors or actresses, see my books **24 Tandem Bible Storyscripts for Children's Ministry** (Standard Publishing, 2003) and **24 Tandem Bible Hero Storyscripts for Children's Ministry** (Standard Publishing, 2003). For more QuickSkits, see **30 New Testament QuickSkits for Kids** (Standard Publishing, 2004).

How to Write Your Own QuickSkits

Begin with prayer. Pray that God will guide and direct your efforts to present his word in a unique, creative, and memorable way. Pray also that the students will be drawn closer to him as a result of your work. And remember, God always hears and answers prayers that promote his kingdom.

Then become familiar with the Bible story you wish to retell. Strive to understand the framework and the structure of the story. Ask yourself: *Who are the main characters? What is the struggle or problem presented in the story? What do the characters learn as a result of facing that struggle? How are their lives different at the end of the story from the way they were at the beginning?*

Keep an eye out for the naturally occurring dialogue in the story. Typically, you'll want to find stories with lots of dialogue. Stories with lots of action or long sections of narration are more difficult to adapt into a QuickSkit.

Ideally, try to find ways to keep all of your readers involved throughout the story so that they don't just stand there, read one or two lines, and then sit down.

Remember that every story needs tension. If nothing goes wrong, you don't have a story, only a list of events. So try to find the struggle or problem at the heart of the Bible story you're retelling and let this struggle drive your story forward.

Look for shifts in time and place as you study the story. Look for repetition (to include) and for things that just don't seem to fit (to exclude). Consider how you'll approach story sections that may not be age-appropriate for your students. Are those sections integral to the story? Can you still be faithful to the text (and tell the story as God wants it told) by leaving out those sections? Violent or graphic sections can be left out completely, or can be dealt with by exaggeration or humor.

Pay special attention to where the story starts and ends. Be aware that it might not mesh with the chapter and section breaks in your Bible. Read the sections preceding and following the story to make sure that you understand the story within its context.

Once you're familiar with the story you wish to retell, begin working on a first draft of your story. Jot down ideas as you say the story aloud rather than trying to listen to it all in your head or furiously write it all out on paper right away. Focus on speaking the story into existence.

Then begin a rough draft of the story. But once again, don't get too attached to the first draft.

Avoid the temptation to "polish" your story too early in the process of developing it. Since the story is being written to be told aloud rather than read silently, it's important to say the words so that you can understand how they flow together, when pauses and interruptions naturally occur, and whether or not the pace of the story is effective.

Recruit some volunteers to help "test-drive" your story by reading the different parts aloud. Finally, as you write your story, remember:

1. Brevity.

Only include dialogue that moves the story forward. Remove all unnecessary words. Make each person's lines brief. Eliminate long sections of one person talking without a break. That can get boring fast.

2. Succinctness.

Change long narrative sections into dialogue. Rather than having a narrator explain all the action, have the people talk about it as they do it.

3. Clarity.

Help the listeners keep track of who the characters are. For example, the Narrator could say, "And then Moses went to talk with Aaron . . . " That cues the audience that the next speaker will probably be Moses. Also, by letting your actors call the other story characters by name, the listeners will more easily be able to follow the story.

4. Simplicity.

Be aware of your word choice. Avoid words or phrases that your children aren't familiar with, or that they might stumble over as they read the script aloud.

5. Naturalness.

Make the language informal and casual rather than stiff and "proper-sounding."

6. Consistency.

Be sure that each character's personality is revealed through her choice of words. Then verify that her character remains consistent throughout the story. Include memorable phrases, clichés, or mannerisms for each character.

7. Humor.

Use humor, but don't overdo it. Move the story along; don't stall out "trying to be funny." Be serious when making an important point or drawing to the close of the lesson.

8. Tone.

Let the tone of your story reflect the narrative tone of the Bible story. Some stories are serious (for example, there's nothing funny about the cannibalism in the "Siege of Samaria"), and other stories lend themselves well to humor. Often stories that are ironic or absurd (for example, Balaam being more stubborn than the donkey in "Balaam and the Talking Donkey") naturally lend themselves to the use of humor.

9. Movement.

While you work on your script, explore your blocking (i.e. where you might stand or move during the story), gestures, and props. You may discover some creative ideas that you can add to your script. Let the story grow as you discover new movement, costume, and audience participation ideas that might add to the presentation.

10. Surprise.

Let your readers do or say unexpected things in order to snag and keep the attention of listeners. If things become too predictable, your listeners will lose interest.

EVE: THE APPLE OF ADAM'S EYE

BASED ON:	Genesis 2
BIG IDEA:	When God saw that Adam was lonely, he created Eve to be his companion. Even with God, we can still be lonely for others. God made us to live together in families.
BACKGROUND:	God spoke the world into existence and called everything that he had made "good." After Adam realized that there was no partner or companion for him, he felt lonely. The first thing that God ever said wasn't good about his creation was Adam's loneliness. God then created Eve from a rib in Adam's side. At last God had finished his creation and he called it all "very good."
NEW TESTAMENT CONNECTION:	God created us to live in community with each other. We're designed to both need and help each other. Believers are told to love each other (1 Peter 1:22; 1 John 4:11; Romans 13:8), accept one another (Romans 15:7), serve one another (Galatians 5:13), be kind to one another (Ephesians 4:32), forgive one another (Colossians 3:13), and encourage one another (Hebrews 3:13).
CAST:	You'll need 4 children for this QuickSkit: Narrator (girl or boy), Eve (preferably a girl), Adam (preferably a boy), God (boy)
PROPS:	None
TOPICS:	Creation, family relationships, friendship, loneliness, new life
TIPS:	Position the Narrator in the center of the stage with Adam on one side and God and Eve on the other. Bring up the stage lights, and then begin when the listeners are quiet.

Director: Lights! . . . Camera! . . . Action!

Narrator: When God was creating the world, all types of fish and birds and animals appeared.

God: Let there be hippos!

Narrator: Poof! There were hippos!

God: Let there be butterflies!

Narrator: Poof! There were butterflies!

God: Let there be a moon!

Narrator: Wham! There was the moon!

God: Let there be all kinds of cool stuff!

Narrator: Zowie! There was all kinds of cool stuff!

God: *(Smiling and nodding)* That's good. . . .

Narrator: But God hadn't made any animals that could talk to him or walk with him, or understand right from wrong, or imagine or dream or believe in him as their Savior—

God:	Hm . . . I'm not quite done yet. I'm gonna make someone special!
Narrator:	So God came down to the earth and reached into the soil and formed a person.
God:	I'll make a man out of mud.
Adam:	That's me—Mud Man!
Narrator:	No, you're Adam.
Adam:	*(Acting like Superman)* Da-da-da-da! Adam Man! Otherwise known as Dirt Dude! Hey, can I have a crime-fighting superhero suit?
Narrator:	Adam wasn't a superhero. But he was pretty super. He had no sin in his life, and he was very smart.
Adam:	E equals MC squared. . . . Wichita is the capital of Kansas. . . . The average rainfall in the southern highlands of Guatemala is 52 inches per year. . . .
Narrator:	And then, God breathed onto his creation . . .
God:	*(Breathe on Adam)*
Adam:	Um . . . did God have bad breath?
Narrator:	No.
Adam:	OK. Just checking. . . . Hey, why didn't he call me "Clay"? That would have been appropriate.
Narrator:	"Adam" means "from the land."
Adam:	I am Land Man! Do I get a trusty sidekick named "Soil Boy"?
Narrator:	Adam didn't have a trusty sidekick— yet.
God:	There! Now I'm almost done with my creation. . . .
Narrator:	Now God was no longer alone. He had Adam to stay with him and play with him and walk with him and talk with him—
Adam:	—a human walkie-talkie—
Narrator:	—and God gave Adam the job of taking care of the beautiful new world.
God:	Adam, take care of the beautiful new world.
Adam:	Okee-dokee, God.
Narrator:	Then, God let Adam name the animals. So God sent them past, and Adam gave them names . . .
Adam:	Betsy . . . Fred . . . Gertrude . . . Ann . . . Julie . . . Bob . . .
Narrator:	Um . . . not quite. Things like, "Hippo! Dodo bird!" Things like that.
Adam:	Oh. Hippo. Dodo bird. Dinosaur. Oranga . . . Orange mango . . . Orgotango . . . Um . . . Monkey. . . .
Narrator:	But as Adam watched the animals go past, he didn't see any that could stay with him and play with him and walk with him and talk with him.
Adam:	No more walkie-talkies . . . hm . . . these are all nice and everything, but I'd really like a sidekick.
Narrator:	When God saw that Adam was lonely, for the first time ever, the Lord said that something in his world wasn't good.
God:	It's not good for Adam to be lonely! I'm gonna make a partner and a friend for him.
Adam:	A sidekick!
God:	Close enough.
Narrator:	So God caused Adam to get very sleepy. . . .
God:	You are getting very sleepy. . . . Sleepy! . . .
Adam:	Um, no I'm not. I'm not sleepy at all. . . .

Eve: The Apple of Adam's Eye

God:	Yes, you are! I'm God, believe me . . . you're getting sleepy! . . .
Adam:	*(Yawning)* Oh, right . . . sleepy. . . . I guess I could use a little nap. . . . *(snore! snore! . . .)*
Narrator:	Then God took one of Adam's ribs and formed a woman. Then, when Adam woke up, there was a lady lying right next to him. . . .
Adam:	Holy Toledo! Who are you?
Eve:	I'm Eve.
Adam:	Can I call you Mrs. Sidekick?
Eve:	Um, no.
Adam:	What about Mrs. Spare Rib?
Eve:	Not a chance.
Adam:	OK.
God:	Adam, this is your new wife, Eve!
Adam:	Where's my old wife?
God:	You didn't have one.
Adam:	Oh . . . hi, Eve!

Eve:	Hi, Adam.
Narrator:	And then they kissed each other . . . kissy, kissy, smooch!
Adam and Eve:	*(Together)* **NO WAY, JOSE!**
Narrator:	And so, Adam was no longer alone.
Adam:	Cool.
Narrator:	Eve was no longer a rib.
Eve:	Cool.
Narrator:	And God had finally finished creating his wonderful world.
God:	*(Smiling and nodding)* **Cool. And very good. I'd give it two thumbs up!**
Narrator:	And God took a rest while Adam and Eve went off by themselves to go kissy, kissy, smooch!
Adam and Eve:	*(Together)* **NO WAY, JOSE!**
Everyone:	*(Together)* **The end!**

(Smile, bow, and then take your seat.)

Eve: The Apple of Adam's Eye

THOU SHALT NOT BITE!

BASED ON:	Genesis 3
BIG IDEA:	God commanded Adam and Eve to avoid eating fruit from a certain tree in the garden. When they disobeyed him, he showed them mercy and love by promising them a Savior (see Genesis 3:15).
BACKGROUND:	The first words God ever spoke to Adam are, "You are free" (see Genesis 2:16). But Adam and Eve didn't honor God in their freedom. When Satan, taking on the form of a snake, tempted Eve, she gave in. Pretty soon, Adam had joined her in her sin. When God confronted them, they discovered that they would have to leave God's garden, but that he still had mercy for them.
NEW TESTAMENT CONNECTION:	In Romans 5, Paul explains that since sin entered the world through one man (Adam), sin can be forgiven by one man (Jesus Christ). Sometimes in the New Testament Jesus is referred to as the "New Adam" since he was tempted yet never gave in to sin.
CAST:	You'll need 5-6 children for this QuickSkit: Narrator (girl or boy), Serpent (girl or boy), Eve (preferably a girl), Adam (preferably a boy), God (boy), Tree (adult, optional)
PROPS:	A piece of fruit and a rubber snake (both optional)
TOPICS:	Choices, consequences, death, following God, forgiveness, God's love, God's promises, grace, hiding, hope, listening to God, obedience, rebellion, second chances, sin, talking animals, temptation
TIPS:	• If you wish, you can invite a person up to be the Tree. Hand him a pear, apple, or banana and tell him to make his arms into branches. If you choose a man or adult for this part, when the script describes the Serpent being in the Tree, encourage the Serpent to climb up onto the shoulders or on the back of the person playing the Tree. Have fun with this part! • Position the students onstage with the Serpent and the Narrator to the left, the Tree and Adam and Eve in the middle, and God on the far right. Bring up the stage lights, and then begin when the listeners are quiet.

Director:	**Lights! . . . Camera! . . . Action!**
Narrator:	**After God put Adam and Eve in the garden, he gave them instructions.**
God:	**You are free to eat of all the trees in the garden!**
Adam and Eve:	*(Together)* **Cool.**
God:	**But if you eat of the Tree Of Knowledge of Good and Evil, you will die.**
Adam and Eve:	*(Together)* **Bummer.**
Narrator:	**So one day Adam and Eve were walking around and came near the tree that God had warned them about. Hanging from the tree was a snake. . . .**
Serpent:	

	(If you have a person playing the Tree, climb up onto his back or jump up into his arms. If desired, wave the rubber snake as you talk) **Did God really say you couldn't eat any fruit in his garden?!**
Eve:	**Of course we can eat the fruit.**
Adam:	**Cool.**
Eve:	**But there's this one tree we can't eat from, or touch. If we do, we'll die. . . .**
Adam:	**Bummer.**
Narrator:	**Now Eve wasn't remembering exactly what God had said. She was changing it around. And so was the snake!**
Serpent:	**You won't die! You'll get smarter! You'll be like God!**
Narrator:	**When Eve heard that, she took some fruit. And ate it.**
Eve:	**Yummy!**
Narrator:	**And she gave some to Adam.**
Adam:	**Cool! . . . and yummy!**
Narrator:	**But as soon as they'd eaten it, they knew they were going to die . . .**
Adam and Eve:	*(Together)* **Bummer.**
Narrator:	**. . . because they weren't living God's way. Then God came looking for them.**
God:	**Hey! Where are you guys!?**
Narrator:	**But they hid from God because they were ashamed . . . and naked.**
Adam and Eve:	*(Together)* **Ah! Bummer.** *(Cross your arms in front of you like you're covering your nakedness)*
Narrator:	**God told them they had messed up big time.**
God:	**You guys have messed up big time.**
Adam and Eve:	*(Together)* **We know.**
God:	**You're gonna have to leave the garden . . . and you're gonna die.**
Adam and Eve:	*(Together)* **Bummer.**
Narrator:	**But then, God promised them a Savior.**
Adam and Eve:	*(Together)* **Cool.**
Narrator:	**That Savior would be their only hope to be close to God again.**
Adam:	**Yummy!**
Narrator:	**Um . . . it wasn't yummy. It was cool.**
Adam:	**Oh. Cool!**
Narrator:	**And ever since then, believing in him has been the only hope for us, too.**
Everyone:	*(Together)* **The end!**

(Smile, bow, and then take your seat.)

Thou Shalt Not Bite!

NOAH AND THE ZOO CRUISE

BASED ON: Genesis 6–9

BIG IDEA: God kept his promise to rescue Noah and his family from the world-wide flood. God keeps his promises to us today, too.

BACKGROUND: After God created the world, the people soon turned away from him. The rebellion on the earth became so bad that God decided to destroy his new world with a cataclysmic flood. However, Noah and his family trusted and followed God.

God told Noah to build an ark. Then, God sent him two of each of the different types of animals in the world so that he could rescue them.

NEW TESTAMENT CONNECTION: Because of his faith in God, Noah was recognized by God as righteous (see Hebrews 11:7). God is grieved by sin and judges it, but is also gracious to those who love him.

Also, in his letter to the early Christian church, Peter explains that the water of the flood symbolizes God's saving power through baptism (1 Peter 3:18-21).

CAST: You'll need 5 children for this QuickSkit: Narrator (girl or boy), Sound Effects Person (girl or boy), Noah's Wife (preferably a girl), Noah (preferably a boy), God (boy)

PROPS: A brown paper lunch bag (or an airplane barf bag); a bottle of bubbles and a bubble blower, or a spray bottle (all optional)

TOPICS: Anger, creation, faith, faithfulness, following God, God's power, God's promises, listening to God, obedience, second chances, sin

TIPS:
- You may wish to let the Sound Effects Person practice his lines before performing the drama. You may also want to give him a microphone (if you have a sound system). Sound effects always sound better through a microphone! Give the lunch bag to the Sound Effects Person (he will hand it to Noah's Wife when she starts to get seasick). And give him the bottle of bubbles (or spray bottle), too.
- Position the Narrator and Sound Effects Person on the left side of the stage, Noah and Noah's Wife in the center, and God on the right side of the stage. Bring up the stage lights, and then begin when the students are quiet.

Director: **Lights! . . . Camera! . . . Action!**

Narrator: **Long ago, the people of the earth were very mean.**

Sound Effects: *(Growl . . . scream . . . do a mad scientist-type evil laugh)*

Narrator: **What are you doing?**

Sound Effects: **I'm the sound effects person!** *(Make the sound of a creaky door. Then do another mad scientist-type evil laugh)*

Narrator: *(Rolling your eyes)* **Oh, great. . . .**

Sound Effects: **This is gonna be fun.** *(Hee, hee, hee, hee)*

Narrator: **People were so mean that God felt sorry he'd ever made them in the first place.**

God: **I'll wipe 'em out and start over!**

Sound Effects: *(Make the sound of an explosion)* **Boom!**

God:	But I'll save Noah, because he believes in me and follows me.
Sound Effects:	*(Very dramatically)* **Hallelujah!**
God:	Hey, Noah!
Noah:	Yeah, God?
God:	Build me a boat.
Noah:	Am I going on a cruise?
God:	Well, sort of.
Noah:	Can I take my wife?
God:	Yeah. Take your whole family.
Noah's Wife:	Oh, goody. I hope it's to the Bahamas!
God:	Not quite. It's a zoo cruise.
Noah's Wife:	Sounds exotic.
God:	Oh, it is, believe me. Now go and get started. . . .
Noah:	Alrighty then!
Narrator:	So Noah and his family built the boat.
Sound Effects:	Hammer, hammer. Saw, saw . . . Hammer, hammer. Saw . . .
Noah's Wife:	Noah, where should I put the sail?
Noah:	It's not that kind of a boat.
Noah's Wife:	Oh. Too bad. . . .
Narrator:	Year after year they worked.
Sound Effects:	*(Act tired)* Hammer, hammer. Saw, saw . . . Hammer, hammer. Saw . . .
Noah's Wife:	This is the biggest boat I've ever seen.
Noah:	It's the only boat you've ever seen.
Noah's Wife:	Oh. Too bad. . . .

Narrator:	Until finally it was done.
Noah's Wife:	Whew.
Noah:	No kidding.
Sound Effects:	You're telling me.
Narrator:	And then God sent the animals. And they came to him two—
Noah:	I know this one! By fours!
Narrator:	What?
Noah:	Two by fours!
Narrator:	The animals didn't come in two by fours!
Noah:	The termites did.
Narrator:	Look, the animals came to him two by two. And Noah and his family packed lots of food because they would have to feed all those animals and themselves.
Sound Effects:	Chomp, chomp. Nibble, nibble . . . Chomp, chomp. Burp.
Noah's Wife:	That's a lot of doggie chow.
Narrator:	They lived with those animals on the ark for a whole year.
Noah's Wife:	That's a lot of doggie poop.
Everyone:	*(Together)* **Yuck!** *(Hold your nose)*
Narrator:	Then the wind and the rain started,
Sound Effects:	Whoosh! Whoosh! Spray, spray . . . Whoosh! Whoosh! Splash! *(Pull out the bottle of bubbles and blow them in the face of the Narrator—or go nuts with the spray bottle)*
Narrator:	Noah and his family and all those animals got on the ark.
Noah's Wife:	Hey, Noah, where's the swimming pool?
Noah:	It's not that kind of boat!

Noah and the Zoo Cruise

Noah's Wife:	**Oh. Too bad. . . .**
Narrator:	**At last, they were all onboard and God shut the door.**
Sound Effects:	**Slam!**
God:	**Hey, that's my line. Slam!**
Noah's Wife:	**Ouch!** *(Hop around on one foot)*
Narrator:	**God didn't shut the door on Noah's wife's foot!**
Noah's Wife:	*(Stop hopping around)* **Oh. Too bad. . . .**
Noah:	**No, it was good!**
Noah's Wife:	**Oh. Too good!**
Narrator:	**And the ark floated up on the water.**
Sound Effects:	**Whoosh! Whoosh! Spray, spray . . . Whoosh! Whoosh! Splash!** *(Pull out the bottle of bubbles and blow them in the face of the Narrator again)*
Noah's Wife:	**Whee! Whee!**
Narrator:	**The ark rolled back and forth on the waves.**
Noah's Wife:	**Uh-oh.**
Narrator:	**What?**
Noah's Wife:	**I'm getting sea sick.**
Sound Effects:	*(Hand her the brown lunch bag)*
Noah's Wife:	**Thanks.** *(Turn your back to the audience and bend over, pretend to throw up)*
Sound Effects:	*(Make gross throw up sounds)*
Noah's Wife:	*(Turn and face the audience again, then say)* **Aah . . . much better.**
Narrator:	**For a whole year they lived on that zoo cruise . . . with all those animals.**
Sound Effects:	**Snarl, snarl. Growl, growl . . . Hoot, hoot. Howl!**

Narrator:	**And they were safe.**
Sound Effects:	*(Gesturing like an umpire)* **Safe!**
Narrator:	**Until they landed on the side of a tall mountain.**
Sound Effects:	**Wham!**
Narrator:	**Softly.**
Sound Effects:	**Oh.** *(Whispering)* **Wham.**
Noah's Wife:	**C'mon everyone! Time to get out!**
Sound Effects:	**Snarl, snarl. Growl, growl . . . Hoot, hoot. Howl!**
Noah:	**OK!**
Narrator:	**Then they sacrificed some animals.**
Noah:	**Let's roast 'em up!**
Sound Effects:	**Sizzle, sizzle. Grill, grill . . . Snap, crackle, pop!**
Noah's Wife:	**Good. I'm hungry.**
Noah:	**Not for us, for God!**
Noah's Wife:	**Oh. Too bad. . . .**
Noah:	**As a way of saying thanks to him for saving us!**
Narrator:	**And God sent a rainbow . . .**
Sound Effects:	**Ta-da!**
Narrator:	**. . . and a promise that he would never let another flood wipe out the whole world.**
Sound Effects:	*(Singing majestically)* **Hallelujah! Hallelujah! . . .**
Everyone:	*(Together)* **The end!**

(Smile, bow, and then take your seat.)

Noah and the Zoo Cruise

BABBLING AT BABEL

BASED ON: Genesis 11:1-9

BIG IDEA: After the flood, the people of the world became proud and focused on making a name for themselves rather than honoring the Lord. We still face the same choice today—will we choose to bring honor to ourselves (in pride), or to our God (in humility)?

BACKGROUND: After the flood, God told Noah and his family to spread out around the world and repopulate the earth (Genesis 9:7). However, Noah's descendants soon congregated in the plain of Shinar (in Babylonia) and settled there.

Then the people built a towering monument to themselves. God wasn't pleased with this show of pride and rebellion, and scattered the people throughout the world. He also confused their languages and, as a result, we have many different languages throughout the world today.

NEW TESTAMENT CONNECTION: At the Tower of Babel, the languages of the world were confused because of the pride of people. At Pentecost (Acts 2) the languages of the world were unconfused because of the grace of God.

CAST: You'll need 4-7 children for this QuickSkit: Narrator (girl or boy), Babbler #1 (girl or boy), Babbler #2 (girl or boy), God (preferably a boy), 2-3 Bricks (boys or girls, optional)

PROPS: None

TOPICS: Consequences, God's sovereignty, pride, rebellion

TIPS:
- Have the Babblers read over their parts and practice saying their lines several times before presenting the story to make sure they don't stumble over the words. If you wish, you could use 2-3 children to be Bricks and form a human pyramid for the tower.
- Position the Babblers next to each other and the other readers onstage as you desire. Bring up the stage lights, and then begin when the listeners are quiet.

Director: Lights! . . . Camera! . . . Action!

Narrator: After the flood, everyone around the world spoke the same language.

Babbler #1: What's happening, man?

Babbler #2: Not much, dude.

Babbler #1: Slap me five.

Babbler #2: Right on. *(Give Babbler #1 a high five)*

Narrator: And everyone understood everyone else.

Babbler #1: I get where you're coming from.

Babbler #2: I catch your drift.

Narrator: Now God had told Noah and his children to spread out and settle the whole world.

God: Have lots of babies.

Babbler #1: OK, man . . . I mean, "OK, God."

God: And spread out around the world.

Babbler #2:	**You got it, dude . . . I mean, "You got it, God."**
Narrator:	**But when the people came to a plain in Babylonia, they all settled there instead.**
Babbler #1:	**We moved into an airplane?**
Babbler #2:	**I didn't even know they were invented yet!**
Narrator:	**It wasn't that kind of a plane. It was a plain, plain. Like a field! And when they saw the area, they said,**
Babbler #1:	**This is perfect for an airport!**
Babbler #2:	**Yeah, the runways could go right over there!**
Narrator:	**No! They decided to build a city there.**
Babbler #1:	*(Rapping, or sing-songy)* **Let's build a city out here on the PLAIN!**
Babbler #2:	*(Rapping, or sing-songy)* **Let's make it pretty and not MUNDANE! . . .**
Both Babblers:	*(Together)* **Dude.**
Narrator:	**Mundane?**
Babbler #2:	*(Shrug your shoulders)* **At least it rhymes.**
Narrator:	**The people used freshly baked bricks to build with.**
Babbler #1:	**Let's make bricks and bake 'em UP!**
Babbler #2:	**Let's mix mud inside a CUP! . . .**
Both Babblers:	*(Together)* **Dude.**
Narrator:	**The people used the bricks to build their city, and to build a tall tower.**
Babbler #1:	**Let's build a tower that reaches up HIGH!**
Babbler #2:	**Let's build a tower that touches the SKY! . . .**

Both Babblers:	*(Together)* **Dude.**
Narrator:	**They wanted other people to remember them long after they died. So they built that tower in honor of themselves.**
Babbler #1:	**Whenever people see our TOWER,**
Babbler #2:	**They'll think of us and all our POWER! . . .**
Both Babblers:	*(Together)* **Dude.**
	(Babbler #1 and Babbler #2 nod and flex their muscles)
Narrator:	**So, rather than honor God, they honored themselves. They thought they were pretty cool.**
Babbler #1:	**Slap me five.**
Babbler #2:	**Right on.** *(Give Babbler #1 a high five)*
Narrator:	**Rather than obey God, they did the very opposite of what God had told them to do. About then, God came down to check on the city.**
God:	**Hm . . . Let's see what those people are doing. . . .**
Narrator:	**But God saw them bragging about themselves.**
Babbler #1:	**Whenever people see our TOWER,**
Babbler #2:	**They'll think of us and all our POWER! . . .**
Both Babblers:	*(Together)* **Dude.**
	(Babbler #1 and Babbler #2 nod and flex their muscles again)
God:	**Oh, no! Look at that! They're bragging and showing off!**
Babbler #1:	**Slap me five.**
Babbler #2:	**Right on.** *(Give Babbler #1 a high five)*

God:	This is only the beginning of what they'll do if I don't put a stop to it!
Narrator:	So God confused their languages so that they couldn't understand each other—
Babbler #1:	Tra-la-la-la! Loopy, loopy.
Babbler #2:	Lappy dappy ding bop!
Narrator:	—they gave up work on their city and their tower—
Babbler #1:	Mungle dee, mungle dee. Moo-ga, ba-goo-ga!
Babbler #2:	Bangy badingo balingy balamb.
Narrator:	—and they finally spread out around the world, like God had told them to do at the beginning. . . .
Babbler #1:	(Walk to the far side of the stage) Tra-la-la-la! Loopy, loopy.
Babbler #2:	(Walk to the other far side of the stage) Lappy dappy ding bop!
Narrator:	And from then on, that place was known as Babel, because that's where the people babbled.
Babbler #1:	Mungle dee, mungle dee. Moo-ga, ba-goo-ga!
Babbler #2:	Bangy badingo balingy balamb.
Babbler #1:	Bangy badingo balingy balamb?
Babbler #2:	Bangy badingo balingy balamb!
Narrator:	And God mixed up the languages of the people on earth.
Everyone:	(Together) The end!

(Smile, bow, and then take your seat.)

Babbling at Babel

5

WHEN SARAH DELIVERED GOD'S PUNCH LINE

BASED ON: Genesis 18:1-15; 21:1-7

BIG IDEA: God kept his promise to send Abraham and Sarah a son in their old age.

BACKGROUND: God had given Abraham a number of promises, including honor, land, descendants, and a future blessing. Abraham and his wife waited a long time to see God's promise of descendants come true.

Finally, God gave them a specific time frame—within a few months Sarah would become pregnant. She found that promise unbelievable, but God fulfilled his promise, making her and everyone else who heard about it, laugh for joy.

NEW TESTAMENT CONNECTION: Just like God kept his promises to Abraham and Sarah, we can count on God to keep his promises to us today (see 2 Corinthians 1:20).

All who believe are spiritual descendants of Abraham (see Galatians 3:6-9).

CAST: You'll need 5 children for this QuickSkit: Narrator (girl or boy), Sarah (preferably a girl), Abraham (preferably a boy), God (boy or girl), Baby Isaac (boy)

PROPS: Dark glasses and a baseball cap

TOPICS: Angels, babies, faith, family relationships, God's love, God's promises, listening to God, patience, prophecy fulfillment

TIPS:
- Since God is in disguise in this skit, you may wish to let the person playing God wear the dark glasses and the baseball cap as a disguise.
- Position the Narrator and God on the left side of the stage, Abraham and Sarah in the center, and Baby Isaac on the left side of the stage next to Sarah. Bring up the stage lights, and then begin when the listeners are quiet.

Director: **Lights! . . . Camera! . . . Action!**

Narrator: **Abraham and his wife, Sarah, didn't have a house.**

Sarah: **No home sweet home . . .**

Narrator: **They just traveled from place to place camping in large tents.**

Abraham: **. . . just tent sweet tent.**

Sarah: **Let's set up camp here, Abe. What do you say?**

Abraham: **Looks good to me, Sarah. Those oak trees will give us some good shade.**

Narrator: **So one day Abraham was sitting under one of the trees near the entrance to his tent when he looked up and saw three men nearby.**

Abraham:	Howdy! Come on in, y'all!
God:	Why, thank you.
Narrator:	He didn't know two of them were angels and one was God himself, in disguise.
God:	Hee, hee, hee, hee. That's me.
Abraham:	Hey, Sarah!
Sarah:	Yes, Abe?
Abraham:	Set out some drinks and fresh bread! We've got guests!
Sarah:	Sure thing.
Abraham:	And let's fire up the grill and throw on some steaks. These guys look hungry!
Sarah:	You got it!
Narrator:	After that, Abraham set out some cold milk for the visitors, and they all sat down for supper.
God:	Thanks for your hospitality, Abraham.
Abraham:	We aim to please.
God:	By the way, where's your wife, Sarah?
Abraham:	Oh, she's in the tent.
Narrator:	Now Sarah wasn't exactly in the tent at the time. Instead, she was hiding nearby, listening to their conversation.
Sarah:	(Softly) I wonder what those three men want?
God:	Well, I've got some news for you, Abraham.
Abraham:	What's that?
God:	Next year about this time I'll return, and you two won't be alone anymore.

Abraham:	What do you mean? Are we gonna get a pet lizard?
God:	No, Sarah's gonna have a baby!
Narrator:	But when she heard that, Sarah burst out laughing.
Sarah:	(Laugh, then say quietly as if you were talking to yourself) A baby! Yeah, right! I'm too old to have a baby. Everyone knows that!
God:	Why did Sarah laugh? Nothing's too tough for God.
Sarah:	Uh-oh.
God:	Like I said, I'll be stopping by about this time next year and you two are gonna have a little baby. You can count on it.
Sarah:	Um, I didn't laugh.
God:	Yes, you did.
Sarah:	I did?
God:	Yes, you laughed.
Sarah:	Oopsy.
Narrator:	Well, time passed and wouldn't you know, God's promise came true!
Sarah:	(Reach over, and pull Baby Isaac toward you)
Baby Isaac:	Waa! Waa! Waa!
Sarah:	Look at that! I had a baby!
Abraham:	Whoa. He's rather big.
Sarah:	He's a healthy baby.
Baby Isaac:	Waa! Waa! Waa!
Sarah:	Isn't he cute! Kootchie, kootchie, koo!
Abraham:	Kootchie, kootchie, koo!
Baby Isaac:	(Loudly) WAA! WAA! WAA!

When Sarah Delivered Gods Punch Line

Sarah:	I can hardly believe I had a baby!
Abraham:	You didn't believe it, remember? You laughed.
Sarah:	I didn't laugh.
Abraham:	Yes, you did.
Sarah:	No, I didn't.
Abraham:	Yes, you did!
Sarah:	I did?
Abraham:	Yes!
Sarah:	Oopsy . . . well, okay, maybe I did. But now I'm really laughing. *(Laugh heartily)*
Abraham:	I'll say you are.
Baby Isaac:	Waa! Waa! Waa!
Sarah:	And I know just what we should call him—Isaac!
Abraham:	Isaac? You know what that word means, don't you?
Sarah:	Yes. It means "laughter" or "joke."
Abraham:	You wanna name our kid "The Joker"?
Sarah:	I wanna name him Laughter. Because at first I laughed because I doubted; now I'm laughing because I believe!
Abraham:	Oh, okay. . . . Then his name will be Isaac!
Baby Isaac:	Goo, goo! Gaa, gaa!

Abraham:	I think he likes his name.
Sarah:	Everyone who hears about this will laugh with me. Because God brought me such joy in my old age!
God:	See, I told you nothing was impossible for God.
Narrator:	And Sarah laughed.
Sarah:	*(Laugh)*
Narrator:	And Abraham laughed.
Abraham:	*(Laugh)*
Narrator:	And Baby Isaac laughed.
Baby Isaac:	Waa! Waa! Waa!
Narrator:	OK, so the baby cried.
Baby Isaac:	Goo, goo! Gaa, gaa!
Sarah:	*(Sniffing the air)* That's not all he did.
Abraham & Sarah:	*(Hold your noses, together)* YUCK!
Baby Isaac:	Hee, hee, hee, hee!
Narrator:	But everyone who heard the story laughed, too.
Baby Isaac:	Goo, goo! Gaa, gaa!
Narrator:	Because God had brought joy and laughter to Abraham and Sarah in their old age.
Everyone:	*(Together)* The end!

(Smile, bow, and then take your seat.)

When Sarah Delivered Gods Punch Line

GOD TESTS ABRAHAM'S FAITH

BASED ON: Genesis 22:1-19

BIG IDEA: Even though God detested human sacrifices, he ordered Abraham to sacrifice his only son as a burnt offering. Abraham was actually ready to do it when God suddenly stopped him. This test showed God Abraham's faith and resolve.

BACKGROUND: God tested Abraham's faith in a remarkable way. Abraham waited for a long time for his son Isaac to be born. Yet, when God gave him the unexpected command to kill his precious son, Abraham was ready to obey. His remarkable faith and obedience serve as an example for all believers, even today.

NEW TESTAMENT CONNECTION: Abraham showed extraordinary faith by sacrificing his son (to God it was a done deal even though Abraham didn't actually kill Isaac—see Hebrews 11:8-19). Abraham believed God would raise his son from the dead because God had promised to send Abraham lots of descendants and Abraham knew God would keep his promise, no matter what. We should follow in the footsteps of this man of faith.

  Even today, all those who place their faith in God are spiritual descendants of this great man of faith (Romans 4:16, 17). Also, just like God provided a ram as a substitute for Isaac, God provided Jesus as a substitute for us.

CAST: You'll need 5 children for this QuickSkit: Narrator (girl or boy), Animal (girl or boy), Isaac (boy), Abraham (boy), God (boy)

PROPS: A sign that a person can wear around her neck that says, "I'm the Donkey!" on one side and "I'm the Ram!" on the other

TOPICS: Faith, following God, God's promises, listening to God, obedience

TIPS:
• The Animal part is purposely brief. Before the presentation, you may wish to point out to the volunteer who plays the Animal that her part is a bit shorter than the others so she doesn't feel bad when she discovers that she doesn't have as many lines as the other children. She should start the skit by wearing the sign so that the words "I'm the Donkey!" are visible to the audience.
• Position the Narrator and Animal on the left side of the stage, Abraham and Isaac in the center, and God on the right side of the stage. Bring up the stage lights, and then begin when the listeners are quiet.

Director:	**Lights! . . . Camera! . . . Action!**
Narrator:	**Abraham and his wife had waited many years to have a baby. Then one day, after their son had grown into a boy, God spoke to Abraham.**
God:	**Abraham!**
Abraham:	**Yes, God. Here I am.**

God:	**Take Isaac, your only son—the son you love—and go to the Mountain of Moriah.**
Abraham:	**Cool! A field trip!**
God:	**It's about 50 miles from here. Then, go up on the mountain—**
Abraham:	**Cool! A camping trip.**

God:	—and offer him as a sacrifice to me.
Abraham:	Cool! A—wait a minute! What did you say?
God:	Offer him as a sacrifice to me.
Abraham:	You mean kill him?
God:	Uh-huh.
Abraham:	As in dead?!
God:	Uh-huh.
Abraham:	Kill my kid?
God:	Uh-huh.
Abraham:	For you?
God:	Yup. You got it.
Abraham:	*(Sighing)* OK, God. Whatever you say. You're the boss.
Narrator:	Now God never really wanted Abraham to kill his son. He just wanted to see how much Abraham would obey. So early the next morning, Abraham woke up his son.
Abraham:	Help me saddle up this donkey, Isaac.
Isaac:	OK, Dad. This is gonna be fun! A trip to the mountains!
Animal:	Hee Haw.
Narrator:	They loaded on the wood.
Animal:	Hee Haw. Hee Haw.
Narrator:	And Abe and his son and a couple of his servants set off on their trip.
Animal:	Hee Haw. Hee Haw. Hee Haw.
Narrator:	It took three days to get to the mountains.
Animal:	Hee Haw. Hee Haw. Hee Haw. Hee Haw.

Narrator:	They left the servants with the donkey.
Animal:	Hee Haw.
Narrator:	And traveled the rest of the way on foot.
Isaac:	Um, Dad?
Abraham:	Yes, Isaac?
Isaac:	We've got the wood here. . . .
Abraham:	Uh-huh.
Isaac:	We've got a knife. . . .
Abraham:	Right.
Isaac:	We've got matches to start a fire. . . .
Abraham:	Yes—
Isaac:	But where's the lamb for us to offer to God?
Abraham:	Well . . . God himself will provide the lamb, my son.
Isaac:	OK, Dad. Whatever you say.
Narrator:	When they reached the place in the mountains that God had pointed out to Abraham, they stopped.
Abraham:	Here we are, Isaac.
Isaac:	Where's the lamb?
Abraham:	God'll provide. Let's get set up while we wait.
Narrator:	So they piled up the rocks, built an altar, and set out the wood.
Isaac:	I don't see any lambs, Dad.
Abraham:	God will provide one. I promise.
Narrator:	Then Abe took Isaac and tied him up—
Isaac:	—um, Dad, what are you doing? Have you lost your marbles?

God Tests Abraham's Faith

Narrator:	And laid him on the altar.
Isaac:	Last time I checked I'm not a lamb, Dad!
Abraham:	God will provide a lamb.
Isaac:	He better do it quick!
Narrator:	Abraham picked up the knife.
Isaac:	That knife looks awfully pointy!
Narrator:	He raised the knife.
Isaac:	*(Weakly)* Help.
Narrator:	When suddenly, God shouted,
God:	Abraham! Abraham!
Abraham:	Yes, God. Here I am.
God:	Don't hurt him. Put down that knife. Don't lay a hand on him.
Isaac:	Whew, baby. That was close.
God:	Now I know that you really do fear me because you have offered me your only son.
Narrator:	Just then, Abraham looked up and saw a ram nearby, caught in the thicket.
Animal:	*(Flip your sign over so that it reads, "I'm the Ram")* Baa. Baa.
Narrator:	He untied Isaac.
Isaac:	Whew.
Animal:	Baa. Baa . . . uh-oh.
Narrator:	And together they grabbed the ram and killed it.
Animal:	Ouch.
Narrator:	And offered it up to God.
Animal:	Sizzle. Sizzle. Sizzle.
Isaac:	Dad, you were right! God did provide a lamb.
Abraham:	I told you he would.
Isaac:	But he cut it a little close there, don't you think?
Abraham:	Isaac, God's timing is always right on the nose.
Isaac:	Yeah, I guess you're right.
Narrator:	And so Abraham named that place "The Lord Will Provide."
Abraham:	Let's call this place "The Lord Will Provide."
Isaac:	Sounds good to me.
God:	Me, too.
Narrator:	And since then, people have said, "On the mountain of the Lord, it will be provided."
Abraham:	Because that was the day the Lord provided for me.
Isaac:	And me.
Animal:	With me. Baa. Baa. Sizzle.
Everyone:	*(Together)* The end!

(Smile, bow, and then take your seat.)

God Tests Abraham's Faith

JOSEPH'S JOURNEY FROM THE PIT TO THE PALACE

BASED ON:	Genesis 37–50
BIG IDEA:	All the while, through the good times and through the bad times, God was working behind the scenes in Joseph's life to bring a blessing to the land.
BACKGROUND:	The epic tale of Joseph sweeps through more than a dozen chapters of Genesis. Through this story we see how God led his people to Egypt and then to the promised land. This drama covers quite a large section of Scripture. It would make a good summary of the story of Joseph.*
NEW TESTAMENT CONNECTION:	Romans 8:28 explains that God still works behind the scenes to bring blessings to his people, *"And we know that in all things God works for the good of those who love him, who have been called according to his purpose."*
CAST:	You'll need 5-7 children for this QuickSkit: Narrator (girl or boy), Brother (preferably a boy), Pharaoh (preferably a boy), Potiphar (preferably a boy), Wife #1 (girl), Wife #2 (girl), Joseph (boy)
PROPS:	None (or an optional sign for Pharaoh/Potiphar)
TOPICS:	Bullies, dreams, family relationships, following God, leadership, listening to God, perseverance, planning, resentment, success, wisdom
TIPS:	• If you don't have enough students for all of the reading parts, you could have one student play both Pharaoh and Potiphar. Make him a sign that he can wear around his neck that says, "I'm Potiphar!" on one side and "Now, I'm Pharaoh!" on the other. Start the skit with the Potiphar side visible to the audience. You could also use one girl to play the part of both Wife #1 and Wife #2. • Also, if you have younger students, you may wish to explain to them that "Pharaoh" was the king of the land, or simply refer to him throughout the skit as "The King." • Position the Narrator and Joseph on the left side of the stage, the Wife/s and the Brother in the center, and Pharaoh and Potiphar on the right side of the stage. Bring up the stage lights, and then begin when the listeners are quiet. *If you're looking for more detailed creative ways of retelling specific stories from Joseph's' life, see the stories, "The Dreamer," "The Rise of Zappo," and "The Family Reunion" in **24 Tandem Bible Storyscripts for Children's Ministry** (Standard Publishing, 2003).

Director:	**Lights! . . . Camera! . . . Action!**
Narrator:	**Joseph had 10 older brothers who all hated him and wanted him dead.**
Brother:	**Joseph's a little twerp. Let's waste him!**
Narrator:	**One day, they were going to kill him . . . but then decided to just throw him in a pit and let him starve to death instead.**

Joseph:	How kind.
Narrator:	However, when they saw some slave traders, they had another idea—
Brother:	Let's sell him and make some money off him!
Narrator:	So they pulled him up out of the pit—
Joseph:	It was the pits in there.
Narrator:	—and sold him as a slave.
Brother:	See ya later, Alligator!
Joseph:	I get the feeling those guys don't like me very much.
Brother:	You could say that again.
Narrator:	The slave traders took Joseph to Egypt and sold him as a slave to the leader of Pharaoh's bodyguards, a man named Potiphar.
Potiphar:	Take good care of my house, Joseph. I'm putting you in charge of everything.
Joseph:	I will, sir.
Narrator:	But soon after that, Potiphar's wife noticed Joseph and thought he was cute.
Wife #1:	(Smiling) What a hunk!
Narrator:	And asked Joseph to make out with her.
Wife #1:	Kiss me, Big Boy!
Joseph:	Yuck! You're already married! That's against God's rules!
Narrator:	But she kept it up day after day.
Wife #1:	C'mon, Big Boy! Kiss me! My lips are burning for you!
Joseph:	You're very gross, you know that?
Narrator:	Until finally, Joseph ran away from her and she got him in trouble with her husband.
Potiphar:	Why were you trying to kiss my wife?

Joseph:	I wasn't! Honest! Trust me!
Narrator:	But Potiphar didn't listen to Joseph; instead, he listened to his wife.
Potiphar:	I'm throwing you in the slammer.
Joseph:	I was afraid of that.
Wife #1:	Bye, bye, Big Boy.
Narrator:	Joseph spent more than two years in jail.
Joseph:	Things just aren't going my way.
Narrator:	But God was with Joseph, and one day the king had two dreams that nobody could figure out.
Pharaoh:	(If you are using the sign, flip it so that it reads, "Now, I'm Pharaoh!") Can't anybody tell me what they mean?!
Narrator:	Someone remembered that Joseph could interpret dreams, so he was quickly brought to the palace to help the king understand his dreams.
Pharaoh:	OK, Joseph! Explain my dreams!
Joseph:	I can't do that, your majesty. But God can. He'll explain 'em to me and I'll explain 'em to you.
Pharaoh:	Funky.
Narrator:	And it happened just like Joseph had said. Pharaoh told Joseph about the dreams, and Joseph explained that there would be 7 years of good weather.
Pharaoh:	That's good.
Joseph:	And 7 years of bad weather.
Pharaoh:	That's bad. What should we do, move to Florida?
Joseph:	No, find someone smart to lead the people. Then have that person save up lots of food during the good years to eat during the bad years.
Pharaoh:	Hm . . . what are you doing for the next 14 years?

Joseph's Journey from the Pit to the Palace

Joseph:	Not much.
Pharaoh:	You got the job.
Joseph:	Thanks.
Narrator:	So when Joseph was 30 years old—
Joseph:	Happy Birthday to me!
Narrator:	—he became the leader of the land, answering only to Pharaoh.
Pharaoh:	Here's lots of riches for you.
Joseph:	Cool.
Pharaoh:	And a wife!
Wife #2:	Kiss me, Big Boy.
Joseph:	Oh, no! Not again!
Narrator:	And after the 7 years of good weather—
Pharaoh:	Ah!
Narrator:	—came the 7 years of bad weather.
Pharaoh:	Yuck!
Narrator:	Egypt was the only place with any food. Joseph's brothers needed food, so they went down to Egypt.
Brother:	I'm starving! I hope they have a burger joint down there!
Narrator:	Well, they didn't know that the guy handing out food was their long lost brother. But when they arrived, Joseph recognized them.
Joseph:	Holy Toledo, it's my brothers! The ones who stuck me in that pit to kill me! That was the pits. . . .
Narrator:	Now Joseph wasn't sure if he could trust his brothers after all those years. So, after a bunch of tests, he finally broke down and cried.
Brother:	Why is that guy crying?
Joseph:	It's me, Joseph! Your long lost brother!

Brother:	Holy Toledo.
Narrator:	Joseph invited the whole family to live with him and they all moved to Egypt.
Brother:	Oh, goody! Can we visit the pyramids?
Joseph:	No.
Brother:	Oh. OK.
Narrator:	And finally, as time passed, the brothers became scared that Joseph would try to get back at them for being so mean to him a long time ago.
Brother:	Oh, Joseph, please don't hurt us!
Joseph:	I won't.
Brother:	You mean you're not mad?
Joseph:	Not anymore.
Brother:	Are you gonna try to get back at us?
Joseph:	No. What you guys meant for bad, God used for good.
Brother:	Is this some kind of a trick?
Joseph:	Nope.
Brother:	Holy Toledo.
Joseph:	It's not a trick, it's called love.
Brother:	I thought it was called Egypt? . . .
Joseph:	I'm saying, I love you and I forgive you.
Brother:	Oh. Cool. That's so sweet! Kiss me, Big Boy!
Joseph:	No thanks.
Narrator:	And so, Joseph took care of his brothers and was kind to them and to their families from then on.
Everyone:	*(Together)* The end!

(Smile, bow, and then take your seat.)

Joseph's Journey from the Pit to the Palace

THE COW AND THE COMMANDMENTS

BASED ON: Exodus 32

BIG IDEA: Moses interceded with God on behalf of the Israelites. Even when they turned from God to worship a golden calf, God was willing to forgive them and stick with his people because of his friendship with Moses.

BACKGROUND: After God delivered the children of Israel out of slavery in Egypt, it didn't take them long to forget about God and falter in their allegiance to him. After Moses had been gone for a long time up in the mountains receiving God's laws, the people became bored and restless. They pressured Aaron into making them a golden cow to worship.

Both God and Moses were furious with the people for their idolatry, and there were severe consequences for the idolaters.

NEW TESTAMENT CONNECTION: God doesn't take idolatry lightly. We may not worship metal cows anymore today, but anytime we're greedy we're being idolatrous (see Colossians 3:5).

CAST: You'll need 6 children for this QuickSkit: Narrator (girl or boy), Israelite #1 (girl or boy), Israelite #2 (girl or boy), Moses (preferably a boy), Aaron (preferably a boy), God (boy)

PROPS: A small plastic cow spray painted gold, a paper bag large enough to hold the cow with the word "FIRE" printed on the side, (optional—cheap earrings or another small trinket to hand out to the audience)

TOPICS: Anger, consequences, disappointment, following God, God's Word, listening to God, obedience, rebellion, second chances, sin, worship

TIPS:
- Before the drama begins, put the cow in the paper bag and place it on the floor or on a table near Aaron. If you wish to make the story more interactive, hand out earrings (or another small trinket) to the audience prior to the presentation.
- Make sure that you explain to all the children that the kids playing the part of the Israelites aren't really praying to a false god; they're just saying their lines and pretending to be like the people long ago who didn't love the Lord. Help the audience and the readers understand that there's a difference between acting in a skit and doing something in real life.
- Since this is one of the longest dramas in this collection, you may wish to practice it a couple of times before presenting it to the other students. That way, you can iron out the transitions and make sure everyone is ready to read their parts. You could also split it in half. If you do, note that Moses doesn't have a speaking part in the first half of the drama.
- Position the Narrator in the center, Aaron and the Israelites on the left side of the stage, and Moses and God on the right side of the stage. Bring up the stage lights, and then begin when the listeners are quiet.

Director: **Lights! . . . Camera! . . . Action!**

Narrator: **After God led his people out of slavery in Egypt, Moses went up on a mountain to get God's rules for the people.**

Israelite #1: **I wonder what's taking him so long.**

Israelite #2: **Who knows? Maybe he got lost or died up there or something.**

Israelite #1:	I'm sick of waiting.
Israelite #2:	Me, too . . . hey, Aaron!
Aaron:	Yes?
Israelite #1:	Make us some gods to lead us.
Aaron:	Make you some gods?
Israelite #2:	Yeah. We're tired of waiting around for Moses and his God!
Israelite #1:	And besides, we don't even know what's happened to Moses!
Both Israelites:	*(Together)* We want new gods! We want new gods!
Narrator:	Aaron was surprised by their request.
Aaron:	Holy cow.
Israelite #1:	That sounds good to us!
Both Israelites:	*(Together)* We want a holy cow! We want a holy cow!
Aaron:	Alright, look. Go to your families and gather all the golden earrings.
Israelite #2:	Then what?
Aaron:	Bring 'em back here to me. I'll show you what I'm going to do.
Israelite #1:	OK, let's go!
Narrator:	So the people did as Aaron said. *(If you distributed the earrings to the audience, the Israelites should go around and collect them at this time)* They went to their families and friends and gathered all the golden earrings and brought them back to Aaron.
Aaron:	Thanks.
Israelite #1:	Now what?

Aaron:	Well, I'm gonna melt them down in this fire . . . *(Put the earrings into the bag)* . . . and shape them into . . . *(Stick your hands in the bag and pretend to shape a cow, then pull out the spray painted cow)* . . . a golden cow!
Israelite #2:	Holy cow.
Aaron:	Exactly.
Israelite #1:	We're gonna worship a metal cow?
Aaron:	Sure, why not?
Israelite #2:	OK, if you say so. . . .
Aaron:	I do! Here you go! *(Hold up the golden cow)* Here's the god who led us out of Egypt!
Both Israelites:	Hooray! Hooray!
Israelite #1:	Three cheers for the holy cow!
Both Israelites:	*(Together)* Hip, hip, Moo-ray! . . . Hip, hip, Moo-ray! . . . Hip, hip, Moo-ray!
Narrator:	When Aaron saw how excited they were, he thought of another idea.
Aaron:	Hey, tomorrow let's have a party and worship the Lord!
Both Israelites:	*(Together)* Hip, hip, Moo-ray!
Narrator:	Now Aaron was letting these people get completely out of control. Rather than leading them closer to the one true God, he was leading them further away from the Lord.
Israelite #1:	Let's get to bed early. We've got a big day tomorrow!
Israelite #2:	Yeah! Let's go!
Narrator:	So early the next morning the people woke up.

The Cow and the Commandments

Israelite #1:	Time to worship!
Israelite #2:	Hip, hip, moo-ray!
Narrator:	They burned sacrifices and brought offerings to the golden cow.
Both Israelites:	*(Together)* Holy cow! Holy cow! We all love our holy cow! Holy cow! Holy cow! We all love our holy cow!
Narrator:	They ate too much, drank too much, and turned away from God.
Both Israelites:	*(Together)* Holy cow! Holy cow! We all love our holy cow!
Narrator:	Meanwhile, Moses was up on the mountain talking to God. *(You could split the drama in half and take a break here)*
God:	Quick, Moses!
Moses:	What, God?
God:	Go back down the mountain. Your people have done something terrible!
Moses:	Oh, no! What is it?
God:	They've turned away from me and made a golden cow.
Moses:	Did you say a golden cow?
God:	Yeah. And they're worshiping it and saying that's who led them out of Egypt!
Moses:	Holy cow.
God:	Something like that. But it's not holy; I am!
Moses:	Right.
God:	These people are very bad, Moses.
Moses:	I know.

God:	I think maybe I oughtta just wipe 'em out!
Moses:	But if you do that, the other countries will say you tricked us into coming out here just to kill us. They won't learn to love you. They'll all hate you!
God:	Good point.
Moses:	And besides, you promised us this land and lots of blessings. Keep your promises to us, God! Please!
God:	OK, I won't wipe 'em out. I promise. But go down and have a talk with them! Now!
Narrator:	So Moses went down the mountain. He was carrying God's rules on two slabs of stone. And as Moses came near the Israelites, he heard the noise of their wild idol worship.
Both Israelites:	*(Together)* Holy cow! Holy cow! We all love our holy cow!
Israelite #1:	Hip, hip—
Israelite #2:	—moo-ray!
Israelite #1:	Hip, hip—
Israelite #2:	—moo-ray!
Israelite #1:	Hip, hip—
Israelite #2:	—moo-ray!
Both Israelites:	*(Together)* Yaba-daba-doo!
Moses:	Yikes. This is worse than I thought.
Narrator:	The people were chanting and praying to the cow. Some were drunk. Others were dancing out of control.
Moses:	Man, they've gone off the deep end for sure.

The Cow and the Commandments

Narrator:	Moses was so angry to see them acting that way that he took the two stone tablets with God's rules on them and smashed 'em on the ground.
Israelite #1:	Uh-oh. I don't think Moses is too happy.
Moses:	Gimme that golden cow! *(Take the plastic cow away from them)*
Israelite #2:	What are you gonna do?
Moses:	I'm melting it down.
Israelite #1:	But that's our holy cow!
Israelite #2:	Hip, hip, moo-ray!
Moses:	Not any more. *(Hide the plastic cow behind you)*
Narrator:	He melted it down, ground it up into dust, and put it in the water.
Moses:	Here, have a drink of your god.
Both Israelites:	*(Together)* Yuck.
Moses:	That'll teach you.
Both Israelites:	*(Together)* Holy cow. Holy cow. We just drank our holy cow.
Narrator:	Then Moses went to talk to Aaron.
Moses:	What happened here? What did they do to you?
Aaron:	Um, don't get mad at me, Moses. They're a wicked people.
Moses:	No kidding.
Aaron:	They told me to do it. . . .
Moses:	Uh-huh.
Aaron:	Then, um, I had 'em bring me their earrings. . . .
Moses:	Uh-huh.

Aaron:	And I . . . I threw 'em into the fire. *(Hold up the paper bag)*
Moses:	Right—
Aaron:	And out came this golden cow. . . .
Moses:	You threw the earrings into the fire and out came this golden cow?
Aaron:	Yup.
Moses:	That's what happened?
Aaron:	Yup.
Moses:	*(Pick up the paper bag and look inside it)* That's the stupidest thing I've ever heard.
Aaron:	Oh.
Moses:	What do you think I am, an idiot!?
Aaron:	Well, I was hoping . . .
Narrator:	Then Moses just shook his head and asked everyone who was on the Lord's side to step forward.
Israelite #2:	We're on God's side, Moses!
Narrator:	The descendants of Levi stepped forward.
Moses:	OK. Here's the deal. This is God's plan. Punish the people. Kill those who turned from God.
Narrator:	And that day 3,000 people died.
Israelite #1:	Agh! *(Draw your finger across your throat, stick out your tongue and act dead)*
Narrator:	The next day, Moses returned to talk to God.
Moses:	I don't know what to tell you, God. They're very wicked. Please forgive us.

The Cow and the Commandments

God: These people don't want me as their God, Moses. They don't want me as their leader, and so I've made a decision.

Moses: Oh, no. What's that?

God: I'm gonna give 'em what they want. I'm gonna let 'em go on without me. I'm leaving 'em.

Moses: Oh, no, God! Please! Don't do that! If you won't go with us, don't send us on. We need you. We really do!

God: I'm so mad I don't even know what I'd do if I were with 'em anymore!

Narrator: But Moses was God's friend, and he begged God again and again to stay and at last God agreed.

God: You're my friend, Moses. And because of you I won't destroy these people.

Narrator: Then God's power and glory filled the tent where Moses went to meet with God. And the people were amazed at the power of God.

Both Israelites: *(Together)* Holy GOD! Holy GOD! We all love our holy GOD! Holy GOD! Holy GOD! We all love our holy GOD!

Everyone: *(Together)* The end!

(Smile, bow, and then take your seat.)

The Cow and the Commandments

9
BALAAM AND THE TALKING DONKEY

BASED ON: Numbers 22–24

BIG IDEA: God used Balaam, a sorcerer, to bless his people. God can use anyone to accomplish his purposes, even an unbeliever.

BACKGROUND: Fear of the Israelites had spread throughout Moab. The king decided to call on a famous sorcerer named Balaam to curse the Israelites. Even though Balaam showed evidence of real faith, he was in the sorcery business to make a living and was more concerned about making a quick buck than about honoring the living God.

NEW TESTAMENT CONNECTION: Peter mentioned that Balaam "loved the wages of wickedness" (2 Peter 2:15, 16). He is held up as an example of wickedness in both Jude 11 and Revelation 2:14.

Many Bible scholars believe that his prophecy in Numbers 24:17 was the prophecy that led the Magi to seek Christ when the star appeared (see Matthew 2:2).

CAST: You'll need 7 children for this QuickSkit: Narrator #1 (girl or boy), Narrator #2 (girl or boy) Donkey (girl or boy), Angel (boy or girl), Balaam (preferably a boy), Balak (preferably a boy), Prince (preferably a boy)

PROPS: None

TOPICS: Angels, choices, following God, God's Word, listening to God, obedience, stubbornness, talking animals

TIPS:
- Since this script is so word-intensive and has a specific rhythm, you'll want to have the readers practice before presenting it to the other students.
- Position the readers onstage as you desire. Bring up the stage lights, and then begin when the listeners are quiet.

Director:	**Lights! . . . Camera! . . . Action!**	Narrator #1:	**King Balak, son of Zippor, saw what Israel had done**
Narrator #1:	**Moses was their leader when they found their camping spot.**	Narrator #2:	**To all the countries near his land— defeating every one.**
Narrator #2:	**They came from ancient Egypt through the desert, which was hot.**		
		Narrator #1:	**And he was very terrified. His country shook with fear,**
Narrator #1:	**And after 40 lonely years of wandering through the sand,**	Narrator #2:	**For Israel had set up camp . . . very, very near!**
Narrator #2:	**The Israelites were ready to go to the promised land.**		

Narrator #1:	The people of his country came and quivered as they said,
Prince:	This great big group of Israelites is filling us with dread! They're gonna chew up everyone, from here to miles around Just like an ox chews up the grass that grows upon the ground!
Narrator #1:	So Balak son of Zippor, king of the frightened band,
Narrator #2:	Sent messengers to bring a famous sorcerer to the land.
Narrator #1:	The sorcerer's name was Balaam. He was famous for his deeds.
Narrator #2:	He'd talk to spirits or call out curses . . . if you paid his fees.
Narrator #1:	So Balak wrote a letter to the sorcerer that said,
Balak:	I need your help! These Israelites are filling us with dread! Please come and curse the Israelites and make them go away. They're much too strong and powerful; I don't want them to stay. I've heard you're good at cursing, and your curses all come true. That's why I sent this message and my messengers to you.
Narrator #2:	When the princes came to Balaam, he said,
Balaam:	Come and stay the night. I'll ask God what he thinks of this and see if it's all right.
Narrator #1:	But that night God told Balaam, "Don't curse! It is not best! The Jews are all my people, and my people I have blessed!"
Narrator #2:	So Balaam told the princes that God had told him "No."
Balaam:	Return again from where you've come. God said I cannot go.
Narrator #1:	So back the princes went again and said this to their king,
Prince:	Balaam would not come with us. He would not curse a thing.

Narrator #2:	So Balak, son of Zippor, sent even richer men
Narrator #1:	Who promised great rewards to Balaam if he'd come with them.
Narrator #2:	When these princes came to Balaam, he said,
Balaam:	Come and stay the night. I'll ask God what he thinks of this and see if it's all right.
Narrator #1:	And God said, "Balaam, you can go, but only do and say The things that I will tell to you. Don't try to disobey."
Narrator #2:	But thoughts of all that money had filled Balaam's head and heart.
Narrator #1:	And he got really greedy before the trip could even start.
Narrator #2:	He hopped onto his donkey, and they started on their way.
Narrator #1:	But he planned to get that money. He planned to disobey!
Narrator #2:	Then the donkey saw a mighty angel standing in the road.
Narrator #1:	So she left and walked into a nearby field that someone owned.
Narrator #2:	But Balaam, he got angry. He didn't smile or laugh.
Narrator #1:	Instead, he beat the donkey with his big 'ol wooden staff.
Everyone:	*(Together)* **Ouch!**
Narrator #2:	Again the donkey saw the angel. She tried to get real small,
Narrator #1:	And smushed the sorcerer's foot against a great big, rocky wall.
Everyone:	*(Together)* **Ouch!**
Narrator #2:	Again he got real angry. He didn't smile or laugh.
Narrator #1:	Instead, he beat the donkey with his big 'ol wooden staff.
Everyone:	*(Together)* **Ouch!**
Narrator #1:	Once again the angel stood there.

Balaam and the Talking Donley

Narrator #2:	Oh, they were in a pinch!
Narrator #1:	So the donkey lay upon the ground and wouldn't move an inch.
Narrator #2:	So Balaam got all mad again. He didn't smile or laugh.
Narrator #1:	Instead, he beat the donkey with his big 'ol wooden staff.
Everyone:	*(Together)* **Ouch!**
Narrator #1:	Then God did a miracle both strange and quite absurd.
Narrator #2:	He let the donkey talk and use a human voice and words!
Donkey:	Why do you keep on hitting me With your big 'ol wooden stick!? I wish you'd stop that hitting, and I wish you'd stop it quick!
Balaam:	But you have disobeyed and made a fool of me instead! And if I had a pointy sword I'd stab and kill you, dead!
Donkey:	But think back, have I ever disobeyed you once before?
Balaam:	No, I guess you haven't. And I hope you won't no more!
Narrator #1:	Then God let Balaam see the angel with that mighty sword.
Narrator #2:	And Balaam fell facedown before the angel of the Lord!
Angel:	Oh, why'd you take that stick and beat your donkey here today? Your donkey had just seen me and had tried to get away. She saved your life, for I was set to kill you with my sword Because you were not ready to listen to the Lord!
Balaam:	I sinned. I'm sorry. I didn't even know that you were near. Just tell me and I'll go back home if you don't want me here.
Angel:	Go along as before with these princes here today. But say the words I tell to you! That's all that you can say!

Narrator #1:	So Balaam met with Balak and the king said,
Balak:	Go and curse! Make the lives of all those Israelites worse and worse and worse! For money, riches, power, and fame— I'll give 'em all to you, If only you'll agree to curse each and every Jew.
Narrator #2:	But Balaam went to hear from God, and when the talk was done, He came back with this message and with blessing number one:
Balaam:	But how can I curse whom God has not cursed? He made the Jews many; he made the Jews first!
Balak:	Quiet! Don't bless them! Don't say something good! I told you to curse them and curse them you should!
Balaam:	But when God wants to bless, Then I have to confess, I must do what he wants— nothing more! Nothing less!
Narrator #1:	So Balak took the sorcerer to a different hill nearby.
Balak:	Perhaps from here the Lord will let you curse them if you try!
Narrator #2:	Again, the sorcerer went to see what God would have him do,
Narrator #1:	And came back with this message and with blessing number two:
Balaam:	God blesses his people; he helps them to win! They'll beat all their foes 'cause they're trusting in him!
Balak:	Quiet! Don't bless them! Don't say something good! I told you to curse them and curse them you should!
Balaam:	But when God wants to bless, Then I have to confess, I must do what he wants— nothing more! Nothing less!

Balaam and the Talking Donkey

Narrator #1:	One last time the sorcerer listened close to see What God would have him say, and he spoke blessing number three:
Balaam:	Oh, Israel is delightful! It's healthy and it's strong! They'll be great. They'll be honored. This is where they belong!
Balak:	Get out of my sight! Go back to your home! You blessed them three times, so now leave me alone! You've lost all your pay— all your riches and gold. 'Cause you wouldn't curse anyone like you were told!
Everyone:	*(Together)* But when God wants to bless, Then we have to confess, We must do what he wants— nothing more! Nothing less! The end!

(Smile, bow, and then take your seat.)

Balaam and the Talking Donley

THE ATTACK OF THE MARCHING BAND

BASED ON: Joshua 6:12-21

BIG IDEA: God knocked down the walls of Jericho and handed the Israelites a great victory on their quest to conquer the promised land.

BACKGROUND: Jericho was an ancient city that had stood for thousands of years. Many people thought it was invincible. It had walls that were up to 20 feet thick and more than 20 feet tall, so when God led Joshua and the children of Israel into the promised land, one of the first tasks was to conquer Jericho. God's unusual battle strategy proved to everyone (including the Israelites) that God was powerful enough to deliver them from any enemy.

NEW TESTAMENT CONNECTION: Today, Christians don't typically have to battle against reinforced cities, but we do have a strong spiritual foe who is out to get us (see Ephesians 6:12). And, just like the Israelites, our victory comes through our faith in God rather than our own schemes and ideas.

CAST: You'll need 5-9 children for this QuickSkit: Narrator (girl or boy), 1-3 Citizens of Jericho (girls or boys), 1-3 Soldiers (boys or girls), Joshua (preferably a boy), God (boy)

PROPS: Large cardboard boxes to represent the walls of Jericho (optional)

TOPICS: Faith, following God, God's power, God's promises, leadership, listening to God, obedience

TIPS:
- You may wish to have the students act out parts of this story. If so, practice before your presentation so that the children are confident enough to know what to say, what to do, and where to stand or move.
- If you use more than one Soldier, have one of them be the spokesperson and have the others only join in by saying certain words or phrases. In their scripts, highlight only the words you want them to read.
- Position Joshua and the Soldiers on the left side of the stage, God and the Narrator in the center, and the Citizens of Jericho on the right side of the stage. You may wish to have God stand on a chair or stool. If you use cardboard boxes to represent the walls of Jericho, position them between the Citizens and other readers in center stage. Bring up the stage lights, and then begin when the listeners are quiet.

Director: **Lights! . . . Camera! . . . Action!**

Narrator: **Jericho was a great big city with tall, tall walls.**

Soldier: *(Looking up toward the Citizens of Jericho)* **Whoa. Those walls are tall!**

Citizens: **Our walls are tall! Our walls won't fall! You can't even dent our walls at all! Naa-naa-nah-boo-boo!** *(Stick out your tongue)*

Narrator: **But then God spoke to Joshua:**

God: **Josh, I'm giving you this city.**

Joshua:	*(Look up toward God)* **Cool.**
God:	**Here's what to do. Get a bunch of trumpets and then march around the city.**
Joshua:	**You want a marching band?**
God:	**Something like that. Toot the trumpets the whole time.**
Joshua:	**That's a lot of tooting.**
God:	**Yup, it sure is. . . . Then march around the city once a day for six days.**
Joshua:	**That's a lot of marching.**
God:	**Yup, it sure is. . . . Then on the 7th day march around the city seven times. And then, I want all 600,000 of you to scream at the top of your lungs.**
Joshua:	**That's a lot of noise.**
God:	**Yup, it sure is. . . . Then, I'll knock down the walls and you can wipe out the city.**
Joshua:	**That's cool.**
God:	**Yup, it sure is.**
Narrator:	**But the people in Jericho weren't about to give up.**
Citizens:	**Our walls are tall! Our walls won't fall! You can't even dent our walls at all! Naa-naa-nah-boo-boo!** *(Stick out your tongue)*
Narrator:	**So Joshua told the priests the plan, and he handed out trumpets. Then they took the ark—**
Joshua:	**—that's a lot of animals!**
Narrator:	**Um. Not that ark. The ark of the covenant. The one with God's laws in it.**
Joshua:	**Oh, yeah. Right.**

Narrator:	**—and then the soldiers and priests marched around the city.**
Soldier:	*(Chanting and marching like a soldier. If you are acting out the story, the Soldiers can march around the audience)* **Left . . . left . . . left, right, left! . . . Left . . . left . . . left, right, left! . . .**
Narrator:	**Um. They were quiet as they marched.**
Soldier:	**Oh.** *(Mouthing the words and marching)* **Left . . . left . . . left, right, left! . . . Left . . . left . . . left, right, left! . . .**
Narrator:	**They did this for six days—**
Soldier:	*(Talking very fast)* **Left . . . left . . . left, right, left! . . . Left . . . left . . . left, right, left! . . .**
Narrator:	**—while the people in Jericho watched from the top of the walls.**
Citizens:	**Our walls are tall! Our walls won't fall! You can't even dent our walls at all! Naa-naa-nah-boo-boo!** *(Stick out your tongue)*
Narrator:	**On the 7th day they marched around the city seven times, just as God had said.**
Soldier:	**Oh, boy, here we go.** *(Acting really tired)* **Left . . . left . . . left, right, left! . . . Left . . . left . . . left, right, left! . . . Whew! That's a lot of marching.**
God:	**Yup, it sure is.**
Narrator:	**Then the soldiers were quiet while the priests blew their trumpets.** *(Wait . . . Nothing happens. Then say to the Soldier)* **I said the priests blew the trumpets.**
Soldier:	**I know. I'm a soldier, remember?**
Narrator:	**Blow a trumpet already. We don't have anyone playing the priests!**

Soldier:	Oh. OK. Where's my trumpet?
Narrator:	Use your imagination.
Soldier:	Oh. OK. *(Pretending to blow a trumpet)* Toot . . . toot . . . toot, toot, toot! . . . Toot . . . toot . . . toot, toot, toot! . . .
Narrator:	Very nice. And then Josh said,
Joshua:	OK, it's time to shout like you mean it!
Narrator:	And the soldiers and priests all shouted—
Soldier:	Like you mean it!
Narrator:	No, that's not what I meant! I mean they shouted loudly!
Soldier:	Oh . . . Loudly!
Narrator:	Just shout already!
Soldier:	Already!
Narrator:	*(Sigh)*
Soldier:	Timber?
Narrator:	Well, close enough. And then the walls came down!

(God, step off your chair or stool, walk over and knock over the walls. If you are using cardboard boxes to represent the walls, knock them over and throw a few at the people hiding behind them.)

Citizens:	Our walls are tall! Our walls won't fall! You can't even dent our *(Pause and look up as if seeing the walls falling on top of you)* —Uh- oh . . . our walls were tall! Our walls did fall! And they basically smashed us as flat as a pancake.
Narrator:	And the soldiers and priests and Joshua went in and killed the people of the city. *(You could act this part out if you like)*
Citizens:	Agh! Help! *(Fall over onto the ground and act dead)*
Joshua:	That's a lot of dead people.
God:	Yup, it sure is.
Soldier:	Hooray! . . . Hooray! . . . Hooray, hooray, hooray! . . . Hooray! . . . Hooray! . . . Hooray, hooray, hooray! . . .
Narrator:	The Israelites trusted God, they did what he said, and God kept his promises to them!
God:	Yup, I sure did.
Everyone:	*(Together)* The end!

(Smile, bow, and then take your seat.)

The Attack of the Marching Band

THE LONGEST DAY

BASED ON: Joshua 10:1-27

BIG IDEA: God made the sun stand still to give Joshua enough daylight to conquer his enemies.

BACKGROUND: After the battle of Jericho, fear of the Israelites spread throughout the promised land. When Adoni-Zedek (king of Jerusalem) heard of Israel's victories in the Canaanite territories, he put together a coalition of four other kings to attack the Gibeonites, Israel's new allies.

The Gibeonites called on Joshua for help, and God used the event to deliver to Joshua a great victory, even stopping the earth's rotation long enough for Joshua to wipe out the enemy armies!

NEW TESTAMENT CONNECTION: Jesus made the astounding promise that whatever we ask for in his name (and according to his will) he will grant to us (see John 14:13, 14, 16:24-26). Joshua obviously believed this about God, too. So pray big, bold prayers and then trust God to do mighty things!

CAST: You'll need 9 children for this QuickSkit: Narrator (girl or boy), Gibeonite (girl or boy), Adoni-Zedek (boy or girl), 4 Kings (boys or girls), Joshua (preferably a boy), God (boy)

PROPS: None

TOPICS: Astronomical anomalies, conviction, faith, God's sovereignty, prayer, success

TIPS:
- At some points in this drama, Adoni-Zedek speaks and at other times the Four Kings speak. Sometimes, all five of them speak and act together. In those instances, they are referred to as the Five Kings in the script. Point this out to your readers before beginning the presentation so they'll be on the lookout for their specific speaking parts. You may wish to take a highlight marker and highlight the speaking parts so they don't get confused.
- For the Five Kings, choose students who like to ham it up a little bit (without getting totally carried away). These parts are somewhat physical (they fall down and bang into each other repeatedly).
- Position the Four Kings on the left side of the stage with Adoni-Zedek next to them, the Narrator and God in center stage, and the Gibeonite and Joshua on the right side of the stage. Bring up the stage lights, and then begin when the listeners are quiet.

Director:	**Lights! . . . Camera! . . . Action!**	Adoni-Zedek:	**Oh, man. We're in trouble now!**
Narrator:	**Before the Israelites conquered Canaan, another king ruled the city of Jerusalem.**	Narrator:	**Especially, when he heard that the Israelites had teamed up with the Gibeonites, who were mighty warriors.**
Adoni-Zedek:	**That's me.**	Gibeonite:	**That's me!** *(Flex your muscles and act brave)*
Narrator:	**And when he heard about the victories of the Israelites over Jericho and the other nearby kings, he was scared.**	Adoni-Zedek:	**We're in double trouble now!**

Narrator:	He was really scared!
Adoni-Zedek:	*(Bite your fingernails, shake your knees, and act scared)*
Narrator:	I mean really, really scared.
Adoni-Zedek:	*(Bite your fingernails even more and act even more scared)*
Narrator:	I mean, really, really, really scared.
Adoni-Zedek:	*(Fall over and freak out)*
Narrator:	That's what I call scared.
Adoni-Zedek:	No kidding.
Narrator:	So he called in four other kings.
Four Kings:	*(Together)* Yo!
Narrator:	And he told them,
Adoni-Zedek:	Let's work together.
Four Kings:	*(Together)* Yeah!
Adoni-Zedek:	Let's attack Gibeon!
Four Kings:	*(Louder, together)* Yeah!!
Adoni-Zedek:	Let's do it now!
Four Kings:	*(Really loudly, together)* YEAH!
Adoni-Zedek:	10-62-51-23 Hut, Hut, Hike!
Narrator:	They didn't say, "Hut, Hut, Hike!"
Adoni-Zedek:	Oh.
Narrator:	But they did combine their armies and move into position to attack Gibeon.
Adoni-Zedek:	You guys are goners!
Gibeonite:	Uh-oh. We're goners.
Narrator:	So the people of Gibeon sent a message to Joshua,
Gibeonite:	If you don't help us, we'll be goners!
Narrator:	So Joshua led his army out to help fight for the Gibeonites.
Joshua:	10-62-51-23 Hut, Hut, Hike!
Narrator:	It wasn't a football game.
Joshua:	Oh.
Narrator:	But there was a big battle! And God told Joshua he would help him win.
God:	I'll give you the victory.
Joshua:	Cool.
God:	You'll knock 'em all over like Dominoes.
Joshua:	Cool . . . what's a Domino?
God:	Never mind. Just remember that I'm gonna help you win.
Joshua:	OK. Cool.
Narrator:	So Joshua and his army traveled all night and took the enemy by surprise.
Joshua:	Surprise!
Five Kings:	*(Together)* Ah!
Joshua:	Hee, hee, hee, hee.
Narrator:	The enemy panicked. . . .
Five Kings:	*(Jump up and run around in circles banging into each other, falling down and getting up a couple times)*
Narrator:	They fell over like Dominoes.
Adoni-Zedek:	What's a Domino?
Narrator:	Never mind. Just fall over.
Adoni-Zedek:	Oh. OK.

The Longest Day

Five Kings:	*(Fall over, then stand up again to finish the story)*
Narrator:	**Then the Israelites chased some of them along the road.**
Joshua:	**Here we come!**
Adoni-Zedek:	**Yikes!**
Narrator:	**And God sent a hailstorm to fall on the bad guys.**
Five Kings:	*(Rub your head and say this together)* **Ouch.**
Narrator:	**The hail killed even more of them than the Israelite army did!**
Joshua:	**That's a mighty big hailstorm.**
Adoni-Zedek:	**You're telling me.**
Narrator:	**Then Joshua noticed that nighttime was coming. He was afraid the bad guys might all run away and hide in the dark. So he prayed a special prayer.**
Joshua:	*(Praying)* **God, let the sun and the moon stand still in the sky! Stretch out this day so we can wipe out the bad guys!**
Narrator:	**And God answered Joshua's prayer.**
Adoni-Zedek:	**Hey, how come it's not getting dark?**
Four Kings:	*(Together)* **DUH . . . WE DON'T KNOW!**
Narrator:	**Never before and never since has God answered a prayer like that. God was really on the side of Joshua!**

Adoni-Zedek:	**It's almost like God is fighting for those guys!**
Gibeonite:	**God IS fighting for those guys.**
Adoni-Zedek:	**Oh. Bummer.**
Narrator:	**Then Joshua and his men began to head home.**
Gibeonite:	**Thanks, Josh.**
Joshua:	**Don't thank me, thank God.**
Gibeonite:	**Oh, yeah. Right.**
Narrator:	**And then Joshua caught the five kings . . .**
Five Kings:	*(Together)* **Uh-oh.**
Narrator:	**Killed them, and hung their bodies on five trees.**
Adoni-Zedek:	**That's disgusting.**
Narrator:	**You can't say that, you're dead.**
Adoni-Zedek:	**Oh, yeah.**
Joshua:	**That's what they get for being enemies of the Lord!**
Five Kings:	*(Together)* **That's what we get for being enemies of the Lord!**
Gibeonite:	**I'm glad I'm not your enemy, Joshua.**
Joshua:	**Be glad you're not an enemy of the Lord.**
Gibeonite:	**No kidding!**
Everyone:	*(Together)* **The end!**

(Smile, bow, and then take your seat.)

Ehud: The Left-handed Assassin

BASED ON: Judges 3

BIG IDEA: God used Ehud, a clever assassin, to deliver his people when they cried out for help.

BACKGROUND: The book of Judges records Israel's repeated cycles of disobedience, despair, and deliverance. Each time they turned back to God, he raised up deliverers (Judges) to rescue them.

The second Judge was Ehud, a left-handed man who single-handedly outwitted the Moabite guards and assassinated their oppressive king. After Ehud's rule, there were approximately 80 years of peace in the land. You might say Ehud was God's left-hand man!

NEW TESTAMENT CONNECTION: God can use whatever gifts you have to further his kingdom (see 1 Peter 4:10), even something as simple as being left-handed!

CAST: You'll need 6 children for this QuickSkit: Narrator #1 (girl or boy), Narrator #2 (girl or boy), Servant #1 (boy or girl), Servant #2 (boy or girl), Ehud (preferably a boy), King Eglon (preferably a boy)

PROPS: Some big fluffy pillows, a fake sword (optional)

TOPICS: Courage, leadership, planning, sneakiness, success

TIPS:
- If you wish to, you could cover the background information found at the beginning of this skit in your own creative way rather than having the Narrators explain it.
- Before the skit, stuff some pillows under King Eglon's shirt to make him very fat. If you wish, you could give Ehud a fake sword and act out the assassination.
- Position the Narrators together, the Servants together, and Ehud and King Eglon next to each other on stage. Bring up the stage lights, and then begin when the listeners are quiet.

Director: Lights! . . . Camera! . . . Action!

Narrator #1: Once the Israelites had moved into the promised land, God let enemy nations live around them to help his people learn how to fight better—

Narrator #2: And to test them to see if they would keep obeying God.

Narrator #1: —but they didn't pass the test.

Narrator #2: They moved in next to the bad guys rather than living apart from them.

Narrator #1: Strike one. *(Hold up one finger)*

Narrator #2: They married them.

Narrator #1: Strike two. *(Hold up two fingers)*

Narrator #2: And they began to worship their idols.

Narrator #1:	**Strike three.** *(Hold up three fingers, then say)* **You're out!**
Narrator #2:	**So God let the country of Aram take over Israel.**
Narrator #1:	**For 8 years they had to serve that king. Then they asked God for help.**
Narrator #2:	**Help!**
Narrator #1:	**So, God sent his Spirit on Othniel, Caleb's younger brother, who led a war against Aram.**
Narrator #2:	**Hooray!**
Narrator #1:	**God helped the Israelites win and there were 40 years of peace in the land.**
Narrator #2:	*(Smiling)* **Ah! Cool!**
Narrator #1:	**Until, once again, the Israelites did evil.**
Narrator #2:	*(Frowning)* **Boo!**
Narrator #1:	**This time, God let Eglon, the king of Moab, conquer them.**
King Eglon:	*(In an annoying, bragging voice)* **I conquered the Israelites! I conquered the Israelites!**
Narrator #1:	**And for 18 years they had to serve him—**
King Eglon:	**Oh, goody! They have to serve me!**
Narrator #2:	**—until the Israelites begged God to help them. And then, one day, a left-handed man named Ehud took the tax money to King Eglon.**
Ehud:	**Here you go, your majesty.**
King Eglon:	**Oh, goody! The tax money!**

Narrator #1:	**Now Ehud had made a sword that was a foot and a half long. He hid it under his clothes and strapped it to his right thigh where no one would look for it.**
Narrator #2:	**Because in those days, few people were left-handed and everyone wore their swords on their left side so that they could draw them with their right hands. But not Ehud!**
Narrator #1:	**Now King Eglon was very fat.**
King Eglon:	**Oh, goody! I'm fat!**
Ehud:	**Now there's a lot of money there, your majesty.**
King Eglon:	**Oh, goody! I can buy lots of candy bars with this!**
Narrator #2:	**Then Ehud sent his helpers home and whispered to the king,**
Ehud:	*(Whispering)* **I have a secret message for you, your majesty.**
King Eglon:	**Oh, goody! A secret message!**
Ehud:	*(Still whispering)* **But it's only for you.**
King Eglon:	**Oh, goody! It's just for me. . . . Quiet everyone! Clear the room!**
Narrator #1:	**Everyone else left them alone.**
Ehud:	**It's a message from God!**
King Eglon:	**Oh, goody! A message from God!**
Narrator #2:	**The king stood up—**
Narrator #1:	**—which wasn't easy for him to do because he was so fat—**
King Eglon:	**Ugh.**

(Ehud and King Eglon can act this part out as the Narrator explains it)

Ehud: The Left-handed Assassin

Narrator #2:	As he did, Ehud reached down and pulled out his sword and stuck it deep into the king's fat belly.
King Eglon:	Oh, Mama. That's gotta hurt.
Narrator #1:	Even the handle sank into the fat.
King Eglon:	I shoulda laid off those candy bars.
Narrator #2:	The fat closed in over the blade and Ehud didn't pull it out.
King Eglon:	Um. Help? *(Stick out your tongue and make gross sounds like you're dying)*
Narrator #1:	Then Ehud snuck away by climbing down a pipe and crawling through the sewers.
Ehud:	Whew! *(Wave your hand in front of your nose)* This place could use an air freshener!
Narrator #2:	Meanwhile, the king's servants waited and waited for him.
Servant #1:	It must be a long secret message.
Servant #2:	Yeah, no kidding.
Narrator #1:	They waited and waited and waited.
Servant #1:	Maybe the king is in the bathroom or something.
Servant #2:	If he is, he sure is taking his time.
Narrator #2:	Finally, they were so embarrassed they got a key and unlocked the door.
Servant #1:	Oh, boy. He doesn't look too good.
Servant #2:	No, he doesn't. We're gonna need a coffin the size of a Plymouth minivan for this one.
Narrator #1:	After Ehud escaped, he traveled into the hill country and blew a trumpet to gather the troops.
Ehud:	*(Make a trumpet with your fingers and toot it)* Follow me! The Lord has given us the victory!
Narrator #2:	So the soldiers captured the narrow part of the river so no one else could pass through,
Narrator #1:	Then they attacked the Moabite army and killed 10,000 of the strongest warriors.
Servant #1:	This is not our day.
Servant #2:	No, it's not.
Narrator #2:	No one escaped.
Servant #1:	Uh-oh. *(Stick out your tongue and make gross sounds like you're dying)*
Narrator #2:	*(To Servant #2)* I said, "No one escaped."
Servant #2:	Oh, alright. *(Stick out your tongue and make gross sounds like you're dying)*
Narrator #1:	God used Ehud to deliver his people.
Narrator #2:	And after that there was peace for 80 years.
Everyone:	*(Together)* The end!

(Smile, bow, and then take your seat.)

Ehud: The Left-handed Assassin

NAOMI'S NEW FAMILY

BASED ON: Ruth 1–4

BIG IDEA: Naomi's life seemed empty and bitter until God brought her a new family and great joy.

BACKGROUND: The days of the Judges were marked by moral and spiritual decay in Israel. However, there were periods of peace and there were people of faith. This story occurs during that time, and we see in it the examples of God's faithfulness and Ruth's faithfulness.

When Naomi's husband and two sons died, she became bitter. But God filled her life with joy and a new family through her young daughter-in-law's marriage with the kindly Boaz.

NEW TESTAMENT CONNECTION: Ruth, a lady from Moab, believed in the God of Israel. God's love and forgiveness are for all people regardless of their background, lineage, or ethnicity (see Acts 10:34, 35). Also, Boaz "redeems" Ruth and shows us a picture of Christ's redeeming work for his own bride, the Church (see Galatians 4:5 and Titus 2:14).

CAST: You'll need 8 children for this QuickSkit: Narrator #1 (girl or boy), Narrator #2 (girl or boy), Ruth (preferably a girl), Naomi (preferably a girl), Boaz (preferably a boy), Elimelech (boy), Mahlon (boy), Kilion (boy)

PROPS: None

TOPICS: Anger, faithfulness, family relationships, God's sovereignty, grief and loss, loneliness, patience, second chances, suffering

TIPS:
- The three boys don't have long speaking parts, but they do have fun parts. Get some boys who like to ham it up for these parts!
- Position the Narrators next to each other; Ruth, Boaz, and Naomi next to each other; and the other three boys next to each other. Bring up the stage lights, and then begin when the listeners are quiet.

Director: Lights! . . . Camera! . . . Action!

Narrator #1: Back when there were Judges in Israel—

Narrator #2: —that's the ruler-kind of Judges, not the Court TV-kind of judges—

Narrator #1: —a man left Bethlehem with his family and traveled to Moab where there was more food.

Elimelech: There's gotta be a grocery store around here somewhere!

Mahlon: Dad, are we there yet?

Kilion: I gotta go to the bathroom!

Naomi: Quiet, kids. Your dad is trying to drive!

Narrator #2: But then he died.

Elimelech: *(Draw your finger across your throat, stick out your tongue and act dead, say)* Agh!

Narrator #1: His sons grew up, got married, and then they died, too—

Mahlon:	(Draw your finger across your throat, stick out your tongue and act dead, say) **Agh!**
Kilion:	(Draw your finger across your throat, stick out your tongue and act dead, say) **Agh!**
Narrator #2:	**—leaving Naomi, their mother, all alone.**
Naomi:	**I'm gonna go back to Bethlehem. There's too many people dying around here.**
Elimelech:	(Die again) **Agh!**
Mahlon:	(Die again) **Agh!**
Kilion:	(Die again) **Agh!**
Narrator #1:	**One of her sons had married a woman from Moab named Ruth.**
Ruth:	**I wish my hubby hadn't died.**
Kilion:	(Die again) **Agh!**
Narrator #2:	**So when Naomi returned to Bethlehem, Ruth decided to go with her.**
Ruth:	**Your land will be my land. Your people will be my people. And your God will be my God.**
Narrator #1:	**When they arrived in Bethlehem, everyone started talking about them.**
	(During this exchange, the Narrators address each other rather than the audience)
Narrator #2:	**Can you believe Naomi is back?**
Narrator #1:	**Is it really her?**
Narrator #2:	**I heard it is.**
Narrator #1:	**But could it really be her after all these years?!**
Naomi:	**It's me, but don't call me Naomi anymore. That's a pretty name that means "pleasant," but I'm not feeling pleasant at all. My husband died—**
Elimelech:	(Die again) **Agh!**
Naomi:	**—and then, my two sons died.**
Mahlon:	(Die again) **Agh!**
Kilion:	(Die again) **Agh!**
Naomi:	**So from now on call me Mara.**
Narrator #2:	**But Mara means "bitter"!**
Naomi:	**I know. God has made my life bitter. I went away full, but when my husband died—**
Elimelech:	(Die again) **Agh!**
Naomi:	**—and my two sons died—**
Mahlon:	(Die again) **Agh!**
Kilion:	(Die again) **Agh!**
Naomi:	**—my life became empty.**
Narrator #1:	(To Narrator #2) **She's got issues.**
Narrator #2:	(To Narrator #1) **I'll say.**
Narrator #1:	**So Naomi and Ruth arrived in Bethlehem at the start of the barley harvest.**
Narrator #2:	**Now there was a man living there named Boaz.**
Boaz:	**Hey, everyone! That's me!**
Narrator #1:	**He was very friendly.**
Boaz:	(Go around the audience shaking people's hands and greeting them saying things like, "So glad to meet you" . . . "Really, it's a pleasure" . . . "Very nice shirt you have on there!" . . . "Have a wonderful day!")

Narrator #2:	And he loved God.
Boaz:	**Praise the Lord and Hallelujah! Amen and Amen!**
Narrator #1:	Then he saw Ruth.
Boaz:	**Whoa, baby. Who's that?**
Narrator #2:	The men in the field told him it was Ruth, the lady from Moab.
Boaz:	**Listen, Ruth.**
Ruth:	**Yes?**
Boaz:	**Whenever you or Naomi—I mean Mara—need food, come here to my field.**
Ruth:	**Thank you.**
Boaz:	**Don't worry, no one will hurt you.**
Ruth:	**OK.**
Boaz:	**And if you get thirsty, just go get a drink from the water jars.**
Ruth:	**Well, thanks!**
Narrator #1:	Ruth was amazed by his kindness.
Ruth:	**Why are you being so nice?**
Boaz:	**I think you're cute.**
Narrator #1:	Um, he didn't say that.
Boaz:	**Oh, yeah.** *(Clear your throat)* **I heard you helped care for Naomi—I mean Mara—after your husband died—**
Kilion:	*(Die again)* **Agh!**
Boaz:	**—and his brother and his dad died, too—**
Mahlon:	*(Die again)* **Agh!**
Elimelech:	*(Die again)* **Agh!**

Boaz:	**—and I'm praying that God will show you his kindness, because you showed kindness to Naomi— I mean Mara . . .**
Ruth:	**Thank you.**
Boaz:	**. . . and I think you're cute.**
Narrator #1:	Um, he didn't say that.
Boaz:	**Oh.**
Narrator #2:	Then he invited her over for supper.
Narrator #1:	And he told his farm workers to leave extra barley out for her to gather.
Naomi:	**Where did you get all this barley?**
Ruth:	**A guy named Boaz.**
Naomi:	**I think he likes you.**
Ruth:	**Why do you say that?**
Naomi:	**When a guy gives a girl this much barley, he likes her. Trust me.**
Ruth:	**And he invited me back to his fields.**
Naomi:	**I'll bet he thinks you're cute!**
Boaz:	**I do.**
Narrator #2:	*(Clear your throat)* **Eh-hem . . . So one day Naomi had an idea.**
Naomi:	**Um, Ruth?**
Ruth:	**Yes?**
Naomi:	**Tonight put on your prettiest dress and go meet Boaz. It's time to go on a date.**
Ruth:	**OK.**

Namoi's New Family

Narrator #1:	So, that night, Boaz fell asleep by the barley field. When he woke up, there was a woman lying there by his feet.
Boaz:	Holy Toledo.
Ruth:	Hi.
Boaz:	Who are you?
Ruth:	It's me, Ruth!
Boaz:	Oh.
Ruth:	Wanna get married?
Boaz:	OK.
Narrator #2:	Then he gave her six scoops of barley and she went home to Naomi.
Naomi:	Well, how'd it go?
Ruth:	Pretty good, I guess. Look at all this barley he gave me!
Naomi:	Honey, this guy is smitten. By the end of the day, wedding bells are gonna chime!
Narrator #1:	So Boaz planned the wedding, and soon they were married.
	(Elimelech , Mahlon, and Kilion hum "Here Comes the Bride")
Narrator #2:	Soon they had a baby boy.
Boaz:	That was fast.
Ruth:	I've been pregnant for 9 months, Boaz.

Boaz:	Oh, yeah. I forgot.
Narrator #1:	And the women of the town all went to Naomi and said, "Look! God has given Ruth a baby and you can help raise him!"
Naomi:	Yeah, I guess so.
Narrator #2:	So your life's not empty any more!
Naomi:	I guess not!
Narrator #1:	And so Naomi cared for the baby as if he were her own son, even though, of course, her sons were dead—
Mahlon:	*(Die again)* Agh!
Kilion:	*(Die again)* Agh!
Narrator #2:	—and so was her husband.
Elimelech:	*(Die again)* Agh!
Narrator #1:	And when that little baby grew up, he became the grandpa of King David.
Narrator #2:	And an ancestor of another famous baby—
Everyone:	*(Together)* JESUS!
Narrator #1:	And after that, Ruth and Boaz lived happily ever after.
Everyone:	*(Together)* The end!

(Smile, bow, and then take your seat.)

THE VOICE IN THE NIGHT

BASED ON: 1 Samuel 3

BIG IDEA: Samuel learned to listen to God's voice and share what God had to say. He became one of God's greatest spokespersons.

BACKGROUND: Samuel was the long-awaited son of a prayerful woman named Hannah. Since she had promised to dedicate him to the Lord, she took him to the worship tent while he was still a young boy, and he began to live there. Samuel helped the aging priest Eli with the chores since his eyesight was failing.

Now God had warned Eli that he should do a better job of disciplining his sons or there would be severe consequences (1 Samuel 2:27-36). Then one night God spoke to Samuel and, after some confusion about who was talking to him, he listened. The next morning he delivered God's word to Eli even though he knew it was news he wouldn't want to hear. Consequently, Samuel became one of God's most trusted and faithful prophets.

NEW TESTAMENT CONNECTION: When we hear God speak to us through the Bible, we should listen and obey as well. And we should tell others about what God has to say, even if it's news they might not want to hear: "For we cannot help speaking about what we have seen and heard" (Acts 4:20).

CAST: You'll need 4-5 children for this QuickSkit: 1-2 Narrators (girls or boys), Eli (preferably a boy), Samuel (preferably a boy), God (boy)

PROPS: None

TOPICS: Calling, consequences, family relationships, following God, God's Word, leadership, listening to God, obedience

TIPS:
- You can have two Narrators for this drama, or you may choose to just have one child read all of the Narrators' parts.
- Position Eli on the opposite side of the stage from Samuel. Throughout the skit, whenever Samuel runs over to talk with Eli, he has to cross the entire stage! God and the Narrator can be positioned in center stage. Bring up the stage lights, and then begin when the listeners are quiet.

Director:	**Lights! . . . Camera! . . . Action!**
Narrator #1:	**When Samuel was a boy, a priest named Eli took care of him.**
Narrator #2:	**And Samuel helped Eli with his work since Eli didn't have very good eyesight.**
Eli:	**Time for beddy-bye, Samuel!**

Samuel:	**Can't I stay up a little later? Please? Pretty please?**
Eli:	**Nope. Now go to bed.**
Narrator #1:	**Now in those days, God didn't reveal himself to his people very often. Messages from God were very rare.**
Eli:	**Nighty-night, Samuel!**

The Voice in the Night

Samuel:	Nighty-night, Eli.	Narrator #2:	So Samuel went back to bed.
Narrator #2:	So that night, the lamps were burning and everyone was in bed, when suddenly Samuel heard his name.	Samuel:	*(Walk back across the stage)*
		God:	Samuel! Samuel!
God:	Samuel! Samuel!	Samuel:	*(To Narrator #1)* Lemme guess, Samuel got up and ran to Eli.
Narrator #1:	Samuel got up and ran to Eli.	Narrator #1:	Yup.
Samuel:	*(Run across the stage to Eli)* Yes, here I am. What is it, Eli?	Samuel:	I thought so. *(Hop up and run across the stage to Eli)* Yes, Eli? What is it?
Narrator #1:	He thought it was Eli since he was the only other person there.	Eli:	What are you talking about?
Samuel:	I heard you calling. What do you want?	Samuel:	I heard you calling my name!
		Eli:	Wait a minute! We're the only ones here, right?
Eli:	*(Yawning)* I didn't call you, Samuel. I've been asleep. You're probably imagining things. Now go back to bed.	Samuel:	Right.
		Eli:	And you keep hearing someone call your name, right?
Samuel:	OK. *(Go back to the other side of the stage)*	Samuel:	That's right.
		Eli:	And it's not me—
Narrator #2:	So Samuel crawled back into bed and closed his eyes.	Samuel:	So you say.
		Eli:	—that leaves only one option!
God:	Samuel! Samuel!	Samuel:	Someone left the TV on?
Samuel:	Not this again!	Eli:	No.
Narrator #1:	Samuel got up and ran to Eli.	Samuel:	Ghosts?
Samuel:	*(Run across the stage to Eli)* Yes, what do you want, Eli? I heard you calling me.	Eli:	No, of course not! God!
		Samuel:	God?
Eli:	I didn't call you, my boy. Now go to sleep.	Eli:	Yes! He's speaking to you. Go back to bed and listen. If you hear the voice again, say, "Speak to me, Lord. I'm ready to listen." Got it?
Samuel:	But—		
Eli:	Go on—		
Samuel:	—I'm telling you I heard my name—		
Eli:	—You're just dreaming. Now, goodnight.	Samuel:	Speak to me, Lord. I'm ready to listen.
Samuel:	*(Sighing)* Oh, okay. Goodnight.		

The Voice in the Night

Eli:	Right. Say that if the voice comes back.
Samuel:	You're sure it's not you?
Eli:	Positive.
Samuel:	I'm not on Candid Camera or anything, am I?
Eli:	No, now go to bed. And what are you gonna say if you hear the voice again?
Samuel:	Speak to me, Lord. I'm ready to listen.
Eli:	Right. Now, goodnight.
Samuel:	Goodnight.
Narrator #2:	So Samuel went back to bed, lay down, and waited.
Samuel:	(Walk back across the stage)
Narrator #1:	Before that night, he had never heard God speak to him. But pretty soon Samuel heard the voice again.
God:	Samuel! Samuel!
Samuel:	OK let's see, how did that go again? . . . Oh, yeah. . . . Speak to me, Lord. I'm ready to listen.
God:	I'm going to do something that will shake up everyone in Israel. I warned Eli about letting his sons insult me and disobey me, but he didn't even try to stop them.
Samuel:	(To the audience) Yikes. He sounds mad.
God:	Well, now his time is up. This is my message—Eli's family has sins that are never going to get washed away.
Samuel:	Whoa. That's some message.
God:	That's all for now . . . nighty-night, Samuel!

Samuel:	Nighty-night, God.
Narrator #2:	Samuel just lay there until morning. Finally, he got up and started his work of opening the doors and getting everything ready for the worship service.
Narrator #1:	But he dreaded the thought of telling Eli about the vision.
Samuel:	What's he gonna do to me if I tell him?!
Narrator #2:	Then Eli woke up.
Eli:	Samuel! Samuel!
Samuel:	Oh, no. Not this again. Speak to me, Lord. I'm ready to listen—
Eli:	No, no, no. It's me this time. It's Eli!
Samuel:	Oh. What can I do for you, Eli?
Eli:	Well, what did God say to you? Tell me everything!
Samuel:	Everything?
Eli:	Yup. Word for word.
Samuel:	Are you sure you don't want to hear the Reader's Digest condensed version?
Eli:	No, word for word.
Samuel:	OK, here goes. . . .
Narrator #1:	And Samuel told Eli everything that God had said to him.
Eli:	Hm. God said that?
Samuel:	Yup.
Eli:	Well . . . he's God. Let him do what he thinks is best.
Narrator #2:	So Samuel grew up and God continued to speak to him.
God:	Samuel! Samuel!

Samuel:	Yes, God?
God:	I've got another message for you.
Samuel:	Speak to me, Lord. I'm ready to listen!
Narrator #1:	And Samuel told the people whatever God said. . . .
Narrator #2:	He spoke God's word to them from one end of the country to the other. . . .
Narrator #1:	He never backed down. . . .
Narrator #2:	And everyone could tell he was a true prophet of God.
God:	Nighty-night, Samuel!
Samuel:	Nighty-night, God.
Everyone:	*(Together)* **The end!**

(Smile, bow, and then take your seat.)

The Voice in the Night

15

CLIFFHANGER!

BASED ON: 1 Samuel 13:15–14:23

BIG IDEA: Jonathan and his armor bearer trusted in God. The Lord used them to courageously turn the tide in the war against the Philistines.

BACKGROUND: Israel struggled for decades with the Philistine armies. During Saul's reign, Israel was at a huge disadvantage since the Philistines kept a tight monopoly on the military technology of the day. That, coupled with their guerrilla warfare tactics and crippling raiding parties, kept the Israelites in subjection.

Then Prince Jonathan (son of King Saul) decided to make something happen. He and his armor bearer single-handedly tipped the tide when they killed 20 men—after scaling a cliff! God used them to deliver his people and give victory to the Israelites.

NEW TESTAMENT CONNECTION: Jonathan and his armor bearer were ready to turn back from their plans if they found out it wasn't God's will (see 1 Samuel 14:8-10). When we find out God's will, we need to be ready to obey it as well, just as Jesus did (see Luke 22:42).

They also trusted God completely (see 1 Samuel 14:6). We can learn from, and emulate, their courage and faith.

CAST: You'll need 6 children for this QuickSkit: Narrator #1 (girl or boy), Narrator #2 (girl or boy), Bad Guy #1 (boy or girl), Bad Guy #2 (boy or girl), Armor Guy (boy or girl), Jonathan (preferably a boy)

PROPS: None

TOPICS: Bullies, conviction, courage, faith, God's power, Jonathan, leadership, success

TIPS: Position the Narrators next to each other, the Bad Guys next to each other, and Jonathan and the Armor Guy next to each other. Throughout this skit Bad Guy #2 talks like a surfer. Bring up the stage lights, and then begin when the listeners are quiet.

Director:	**Lights! . . . Camera! . . . Action!**
Narrator #1:	**Today's story is one of the coolest adventure stories in the Bible!**
Narrator #2:	**Saul was the king of the land, but the Philistines were controlling the land.**
Narrator #1:	**They didn't let any of the Israelites have swords or even hire blacksmiths to make swords.**
Narrator #2:	**In fact, there were only two swords in the whole country!**

Narrator #1:	**That's not many.**
Narrator #2:	**King Saul had one.**
Armor Guy:	*(Pointing to Jonathan)* **That's his Dad.**
Narrator #1:	**And his son, Jonathan, had the other one.**
Jonathan:	**That's me.**
Narrator #2:	**Now the Philistines were sending raiding parties against the Israelites.**

Bad Guy #1:	Let's go get those guys!
Bad Guy #2:	(Talking like a surfer) Radical, dude.
Narrator #1:	They were attacking the Israelites.
Bad Guy #1:	Hi-ya-ka-bung-ah!
Bad Guy #2:	Gnarly, dude.
Narrator #2:	One day, Jonathan was talking to his friend, a young man who helped carry his armor for him.
Jonathan:	Hey, c'mon! Let's go over to the Philistine camp. Let's make something happen!
Armor Guy:	Sounds good to me.
Narrator #1:	Now on each side of the pass was a tall cliff.
Jonathan:	C'mon. Let's spy on their outpost.
Armor Guy:	Right on.
Jonathan:	Maybe God will give us a victory. After all, nothing can stop him. He could wipe them out with a whole army, or with just a couple of guys like us!
Armor Guy:	Let's do it! I'll follow you anywhere! I'll stick with you no matter what.
Narrator #2:	So they headed out.
Jonathan:	Now we'll let the soldiers see us. If they're like, "Wait there till we come to you!" Then we'll stay put and not go after them.
Armor Guy:	OK. But what if they ask us to climb up to them?
Jonathan:	Then we'll climb up and wipe 'em out. That'll be the sign that God wants us to attack them!
Armor Guy:	Cool.

Narrator #1:	So they approached the cliff and let the Philistines see them.
Bad Guy #1:	Hey. Look at that! The Hebrews are crawling out of the holes they've been hiding in!
Bad Guy #2:	Dude!
Bad Guy #1:	Come on up here and we'll teach you a lesson!
Bad Guy #2:	Yeah, little dudes! We'll teach you how to wax your surfboards!
Bad Guy #1:	Um, that's not the lesson we're gonna teach them!
Bad Guy #2:	It's not?
Bad Guy #1:	No, we're gonna fight 'em and kill 'em off!
Bad Guy #2:	Dude, that's some lesson!
Bad Guy #1:	Come on up here! We'll be waiting!
Armor Guy:	Did you hear that, Jonathan? They told us to climb up to them!
Jonathan:	Yeah, follow me! God has handed them over to us!
Armor Guy:	Cool.
Narrator #2:	So Jonathan climbed the cliff like a rock climber.
Jonathan:	(Act like you're rock climbing)
Narrator #1:	And his armor bearer climbed up behind him.
Armor Guy:	(Act like you're rock climbing)
Narrator #2:	When they reached the top of the cliff, they attacked the Philistines.
	(Jonathan and Armor Guy act like karate experts)
Bad Guy #1:	Whoa.

Cliffhanger!

Bad Guy #2:	Cool moves, dude!
Narrator #1:	And they killed 'em dead.
Bad Guy #1:	Bummer.
Bad Guy #2:	They taught us a lesson . . . dude.
Narrator #2:	In that first attack, Jonathan and his friend killed off 20 men!
Armor Guy:	He did it! God helped us!
Jonathan:	I'll say!
Narrator #1:	The whole Philistine army freaked out. The panic was sent by God.
Narrator #2:	And the men in the camp, and the field, and the outpost, and the raiding parties all ran away.
Bad Guy #2:	Let's get outta here, man!
Bad Guy #1:	We can't. We're dead, remember?
Bad Guy #2:	Oh, yeah. Bummer, dude.
Narrator #1:	Then God sent an earthquake.

Everyone:	*(Bounce up and down, jump around and pretend you're caught in an earthquake)*
Narrator #2:	And he sent such confusion that the Philistines started fighting and killing each other.
Bad Guy #2:	*(Karate chop Bad Guy #1)* Take that! And that! And that! Dudes!
Bad Guy #1:	What are you doing?! We're already dead!
Bad Guy #2:	Oh, yeah. Bummer, dude.
Narrator #1:	And the Lord rescued Israel that day . . .
Narrator #2:	. . . because Jonathan and his friend were brave enough to step out in faith . . .
Narrator #1:	. . . and make something happen.
Bad Guy #2:	That's some lesson . . . dude.
Everyone Else:	*(Together)* It sure is! The end!

(Smile, bow, and then take your seat.)

Cliffhanger!

THE DAY THE BULLY WENT DOWN*

BASED ON:	1 Samuel 17:1-52
BIG IDEA:	David placed his faith (and his life) in God's hands when he faced Goliath. God gave him the victory, and God gives us the victory over the giant problems in our lives, too.
BACKGROUND:	Under King Saul, the Israelites were facing their dreaded enemies, the Philistines. The only problem was, no one in the Israelite army (including Saul) was brave enough to fight against the Philistine champion Goliath. Then David, a young shepherd, stepped up to the challenge armed only with a slingshot, a shepherd's staff, and an unyielding faith in God. Through David, God delivered his people from the Philistines and gave them the victory.
NEW TESTAMENT CONNECTION:	God is on our side today, just like he was on David's side long ago: "If God is for us, who can be against us?" (Romans 8:31). Also, we can learn humility from David's example of giving all the credit for his victory to God.
CAST:	You'll need 6-12 children for this QuickSkit: Narrator (girl or boy), 1-4 Philistines (preferably girls), 1-4 Israelites (preferably boys), David (preferably a boy), Goliath (preferably a boy), Jesse (preferably a boy)
PROPS:	A chair or stool for Goliath to stand on (optional)
TOPICS:	Bullies, conviction, courage, David, doubt, faith, God's power, leadership, success
TIPS:	• You could delete the part of Jesse if you wish to use fewer readers. You could also act out this drama as it's read. Just coach the readers on what to do and where to move. • Position the Philistines on the left side of the stage, the Israelites on the right side of the stage, the Narrator and Goliath in the center, and David and Jesse on the far right. Bring up the stage lights, and then begin when the listeners are quiet.

*An earlier version of this script first appeared in the 2000 Children's Ministry Seminar, "Seven Secrets to Successful Storytelling" published by the International Network of Children's Ministries. Copyright 2000. All rights reserved. Used by permission.

Director:	**Lights! . . . Camera! . . . Action!**
Narrator:	**Long ago, the Israelites gathered to fight against the mighty Philistine warriors.**
Philistines:	*(Together)* **Goliath! Goliath! He's our man! If he can't do it, no one can!**
Narrator:	**Well, if nothing else they were pretty good cheerleaders.**
Philistines:	*(Together)* **Thank you!**

Narrator:	Anyway, the Israelites were on one hill and the Philistines were on another. Every day the biggest, strongest, nastiest smelling Philistine of all, a giant named Goliath, mocked the Israelites and their God.
Goliath:	You measly little worms! I could fight your whole army with my pinky finger! You serve a wimpy king and a wimpy God, and you're all a bunch of chickens! Bawk! Bawk! Bawk!
Philistines:	(Together) Goliath! Goliath! He's our man! If he can't do it, no one can!
Narrator:	The Israelites were terrified!
Israelites:	(Chew fingers and shake knees)
Narrator:	Every morning and evening, for 40 days, the giant would laugh at the Israelites.
Goliath:	(Laugh loudly at the scared Israelites)
Narrator:	The Israelites would shake on the hill, scared to death. . .
Israelites:	(Chew fingers and shake knees)
Narrator:	While the Philistines cheered on their hero. . . .
Philistines:	(Together) Goliath! Goliath! He's our man! If he can't do it, no one can!
Narrator:	One day, a young shepherd named David was sent by his father to take food to his brothers who were fighting in the war.
Jesse:	Dave, take this food to your brothers who are fighting in the war.
David:	Sure thing, Dad.
Narrator:	But when David arrived, he didn't see anyone fighting at all. Instead, he found the Israelites shaking and scared.
Israelites:	(Chew fingers and shake knees)
David:	What's going on? I thought you were supposed to be fighting the Philistines?
Israelites:	(Together) NO WAY, JOSE!

Philistines:	(Together) Goliath! Goliath! He's our man! If he can't do it, no one can!
David:	Well, then I'll fight him. I'm not afraid of anyone as long as God is on my side!
Israelites:	(Together) David! David! He's our man! If he can't do it, we're all dead meat!
Narrator:	The King wished David the best. And David, armed only with a slingshot and a big stick, approached the giant.
Goliath:	Woof, woof, woof! What do I look like—a doggie, that you come at me with a stick? Here, fetch, Rover! I'm gonna step all over you! Prepare to be toejam!
David:	Not a chance, Goliath. You see, my God is a lot bigger than you, and today everyone is gonna find out just how powerful he is when I cut you down to size!
Narrator:	David ran toward the giant and slung a stone at him. It hit the giant in the forehead and knocked him to the ground.
Goliath:	Ouch.
Narrator:	Then David took Goliath's own spear and sliced off his head.
Goliath:	Yuck.
Narrator:	Blood spewed all over and it was really gross.
Israelites:	(Together) EW! THAT'S GROSS!
Narrator:	The Philistines saw it and were so scared they ran for their lives . . .
Philistines:	(Together) Goliath! Goliath! He's our–uh, oh. We're outta here!
Narrator:	. . . being chased by the now-brave Israelites!
Israelites:	(Flex muscles and act brave)
Narrator:	And from then on, everyone knew that the God of the Israelites was for real.
Everyone:	(Together) The end!

(Smile, bow, and then take your seat.)

The Day the Bully Went Down

JONATHAN AND DAVID: FRIENDS FOR LIFE

BASED ON: 1 Samuel 18–20

BIG IDEA: Jonathan and David had a rich and abiding friendship that weathered even the most severe storms.

BACKGROUND: Saul, Israel's first king, became insanely jealous of the young warrior, David, after David's fame began to spread throughout the land. Saul was afraid David would wrench the throne from himself or his son, Prince Jonathan (see 1 Samuel 18:8, 15, 28, 29 and 20:31). Saul repeatedly tried to kill David, but David continued to elude him. This only served to inflame Saul's hatred and irrational fears.

The irony is, as much as Saul hated David, his family loved him. Jonathan became best friends with David, and Saul's daughter Michal fell in love with and married David.

NEW TESTAMENT CONNECTION: Jonathan was willing to identify with David even when it endangered his life. Jesus pointed out the greatest love of all is the love that is willing to give up its life for a friend. "Greater love has no one than this, that he lay down his life for his friends" (John 15:13).

CAST: You'll need 6-8 children for this QuickSkit: Narrator #1 (girl or boy), Narrator #2 (girl or boy), 1-3 Singers (girls or boys), David (preferably a boy), Jonathan (preferably a boy), Saul (preferably a boy)

PROPS: Four plastic drinking straws

TOPICS: Anger, conviction, David, family relationships, friendship, jealousy, Jonathan, loyalty, stubbornness

TIPS:
- During this story, there are a number of times when Saul throws a spear at David and at his son Jonathan. Rather than using real spears (which might be a little dangerous), use drinking straws. Give the straws to Saul before the skit begins.
- Position the Narrators and the singers next to each other on the left side of the stage, Jonathan and David next to each other on the right side of the stage, and Saul in the center. Bring up the stage lights, and then begin when the listeners are quiet.

Director:	**Lights! . . . Camera! . . . Action!**
Narrator #1:	**After David beat Goliath—**
Saul:	**That was pretty cool, by the way!** *(Pretend to use a sling shot)* **Dead as a road-killed possum!**
Narrator #2:	**—he became good friends with King Saul's son, Jonathan.**
Jonathan:	**David, here's my sword and my sheath as a gift.**
David:	**Thanks!**
Jonathan:	**You're my friend forever.**
David:	**And you're mine.**
Jonathan:	**Promise?**

David:	**Promise.**
Jonathan:	**Good. Here's my bow, too.**
David:	**OK.**
Jonathan:	**And my robe and my tunic and—**
David:	**—okay, buddy. Let's not get carried away here.**
Narrator #1:	**But soon after that, Saul became upset because everyone was singing songs about David.**
Singer:	*(Sing to the tune of "Jingle Bells")* **We love Dave. . . . We love Dave . . . more than we love Saul. . . . Saul's okay but Dave's the one that we love most of all!** **We love Dave. . . . We love Dave . . . more than we love Saul. . . . David's cute and strong and smart and Saul is only tall!**
Narrator #2:	**Well, something like that. And so, when David came over to play the harp for Saul, just like he always did . . .**
David:	*(Pretend to strum an electric guitar)*
Saul:	*(Do the following actions as the Narrator describes them, throwing a straw instead of a spear . . .)*
Narrator #1:	**Saul took a spear . . . aimed it at David . . . and threw it at him.**
David:	**Hey, watch it! That thing's pointy!**
Narrator #2:	**And then, David went back to playing his harp.**
David:	**Strum . . . strum . . . strum . . .** *(Pretend to strum an electric guitar)*
Narrator #2:	**It was a harp, David, not an electric guitar.**
David:	**Oh.** *(Pretend to beat on a set of drums)*
Narrator #2:	**I said harp, not drum set.**

David:	**OK, okay.** *(Pretend to strum a harp, but as soon as the Narrator looks away, pretend to beat on a set of drums again)*
Saul:	*(Do the following actions as the Narrator describes them, throwing a straw instead of a spear . . .)*
Narrator #1:	**Once again, Saul took a spear . . . aimed it at David . . . and threw it at him.**
David:	**What are you trying to do? Make me into a human shish kabob?! I'm outta here, dude!**
Narrator #2:	**And when David met up with Jonathan, he told him all about it.**
David:	**So I'm just standing there in the living room playing the harp, and then your Dad takes this spear—**
Jonathan:	**—the pointy one?—**
David:	**—yeah, the pointy one! And he throws it at me!**
Jonathan:	**That explains the hole in the wall.**
David:	**Yeah, well usually people clap when I play the harp; they don't throw spears at me.**
Jonathan:	**Maybe you hit a wrong note?**
David:	**Look, your Dad was trying to kill me.**
Jonathan:	**How can you be sure? Maybe he thought you were a stray antelope or something. . . .**
David:	**Do I look like an antelope?!**
Jonathan:	**I guess not. . . .**
David:	**Besides, he took another spear and tried it again!**
Jonathan:	**Really? I don't believe it!**
David:	**Believe it, buster. Lucky for me he doesn't have good aim.**

Jonathan and David: Friends for Life

Narrator #1:	Then after that, Saul sent David into battle, hoping he'd be killed there.
Saul:	That'll do it. Why should I kill him? I'll let our enemies do it instead!
Narrator #2:	But David just won the battles and fought so well that even more people sang about him.
Singer:	*(Sing to the tune of "Row, Row, Row Your Boat")* Swing, swing, swing your sling Swiftly through the air! David killed Goliath and A lion and a bear! Dave, Dave, Dave is great. Killing more than Saul! Line up all our enemies. Dave'll kill 'em all!
Saul:	I'll get him one way or another!
Narrator #1:	Then Saul told all his servants and his son, Jonathan, to kill David, but Jonathan went to warn him.
Jonathan:	Watch out, Dave. My dad wants to make you into a human shish kabob.
David:	Yeah, no kidding.
Narrator #1:	Then Jonathan went back to talk to his dad.
Jonathan:	Dad, what's the deal?
Saul:	I don't like him.
Jonathan:	But, Dad! He never did anything to hurt you. In fact, he's helped you. He killed Goliath, remember?
Saul:	Yeah, that was pretty cool, by the way. *(Pretend to use a sling shot)* Dead as a road-killed possum!
Jonathan:	And David has helped our country win lots of battles!
Saul:	OK, okay, you're right. I agree. I won't hurt him.
Jonathan:	Promise?

Saul:	Promise.
Narrator #2:	So Jonathan called David back to the palace, and things went back to normal . . . for awhile.
Jonathan:	You're my friend forever.
David:	And you're mine.
Jonathan:	Promise?
David:	Promise.
Narrator #1:	But soon after that war broke out again.
Narrator #2:	David led the army and became a famous war hero once again. . . .
Singer:	*(Sing to the tune of "B-I-N-G-O")* There was a warrior won a war And David was his name-o! D-A-V-I-D . . . D-A-V-I-D . . . D-A-V-I-D . . . And David was his name-o!
Narrator #1:	. . . And Saul just got jealous all over again.
David:	Hey, put that spear away!
Saul:	*(Aim the straw at David and throw it at him)*
David:	OK, that's it. I'm outta here for good!
Narrator #2:	Five more times, Saul tried to have David killed. But every time, David escaped.
David:	Whew.
Saul:	Curses! Foiled again!
Narrator #1:	Then, when David found Jonathan, he told him all about it.
David:	Look, dude, your dad is SO trying to kill me. He did the spear thing again! What's the deal? Why is he so mad?
Jonathan:	What? No way! I'm telling you he promised he wouldn't try to hurt you any more. Remember?

David:	I remember, but I don't think he does.
Jonathan:	Hm . . . well, what should we do?
David:	Look, I'm supposed to show up for a party at the palace tomorrow, right?
Jonathan:	Yeah. To dedicate next month to the Lord.
David:	Well, I'm not comin'. Tell your dad I had to go home for a special sacrifice. See how he acts. If he's cool about it, then I'll come back. But if he freaks out, then you'll know he's out to get me.
Jonathan:	Sounds like a plan.
David:	So how are you gonna get word to me either way?
Narrator #2:	They set up a secret time and place to meet, and then they went their separate ways.
Narrator #1:	And the next day at the party, Saul was on the lookout for David.
Saul:	Hm . . . where is that guy, anyway?
Narrator #2:	When David didn't show up that day, or the day after, Saul asked Jonathan about it.
Saul:	Hey, do you know where David is?
Jonathan:	Yeah, he had to go to Bethlehem for a special sacrifice.
Saul:	What! I knew it! I knew you were on his side!
Jonathan:	Dad, what's the deal with you?
Saul:	*(Screaming like a crazy man)* Aah!
Narrator #1:	And then, Saul threw a spear at his own son—
Saul:	*(Aim the straw at Jonathan and throw it at him)*
Narrator #2:	—and Jonathan knew for certain that his dad hated David.
Jonathan:	No kidding.
Narrator #1:	Then Jonathan left the table and went to the secret meeting with David. He told him how his dad had acted.
David:	See?
Jonathan:	Yeah, well, then he tried to make ME into a human shish kabob!
David:	I know the feeling. Somebody oughtta take that spear away from him and put him on a timeout.
Jonathan:	Yeah, no kidding.
Narrator #2:	But still, Jonathan promised once again to be David's friend forever.
Jonathan:	You're my friend forever.
David:	And you're mine.
Jonathan:	Promise?
David:	Promise.
Narrator #1:	They knew they wouldn't be able to hang out together, or they'd both be in danger.
Narrator #2:	So they went their separate ways.
Narrator #1:	But even though they were far apart, their hearts remained close together forever—
Narrator #2:	—just as it is with all true friends—
Narrator #1:	—even to this very day.
Everyone:	*(Together)* The end!

(Smile, bow, and then take your seat.)

Jonathan and David: Friends for Life

DAVID'S MIGHTY MEN

BASED ON: 1 Chronicles 11; 2 Samuel 23:8-39

BIG IDEA: David's mighty men faithfully and bravely fought on the side of God's armies and helped fortify the strength of David's kingdom.

BACKGROUND: By the time David was officially crowned king, he already had a group of experienced soldiers of fortune who were faithful to him. As his fame spread, other warriors soon joined him. The Bible shares the exploits of some of these "Mighty Men."

Apparently, there were three especially renowned fighters (one of whom was named Eleazar). The leader of this group was a man named Ish-Bosheth, who killed 800 men single-handedly with a spear. These men were known as "The Three."

Then there was a group of 30 more warriors led by Abishai. One of these men, Benaiah, became more famous than the rest of them and was placed in charge of David's bodyguard. Later, under King Solomon, Benaiah became the commander of Israel's army (see 1 Kings 2:35).

This QuickSkit explores some of the adventures of David's bravest heroes.

NEW TESTAMENT CONNECTION: David's heroes were known for their incredible courage and skill. We can learn from them to be strong and courageous, too. "Be on your guard; stand firm in the faith; be men of courage; be strong. Do everything in love" (1 Corinthians 16:13, 14).

CAST: You'll need 5 children for this QuickSkit: Narrator #1 (girl or boy), Narrator #2 (girl or boy), Eleazar (preferably a boy), Ish-Bosheth (preferably a boy), Benaiah (preferably a boy)

PROPS: None

TOPICS: Courage, David, giftedness, leadership, success

TIPS:
- Even though this is the story of the three "Mighty Men," for a humorous take on the story, you may wish to have one or more girls play the part of a mighty man!
- This is a fast-moving skit with lots of actions, jokes, and interruptions. You may want to have the readers rehearse a few times before performing it for your group.
- Position the Narrators next to each other, and the Mighty Men next to each other on stage. Bring up the stage lights, and then begin when the listeners are quiet.

Director:	**Lights! . . . Camera! . . . Action!**
Narrator #1:	**When King David was being chased by Saul, he lived in the desert, and a group of adventurers joined him.**
Mighty Men:	*(Together)* **All for one and one for all! . . . YO!**
Narrator #2:	**Some of these men became David's bravest heroes.**
Eleazar:	**Don't applaud; just send money!**
Narrator #1:	**When David became king, his Mighty Men fought for him, and their fame spread through the land.**
Narrator #2:	**Let's look at the stories of three of David's most famous heroes!**
Eleazar:	**I'm Mighty Man one! My name is Eleazar.**

Ish-Bosheth:	**I'm Mighty Man two! My name is Ish-Bosheth!**
Benaiah:	**I'm Mighty Mouse!**
Narrator #1:	**Um, you're not a mighty mouse; you're a mighty man!**
Benaiah:	**Oh, yeah . . . I'm Mighty Man three! My name is . . . Arnold Schwarzenegger** *(or another popular action hero).*
Narrator #1:	**You are Benaiah.**
Benaiah:	**Oh . . . I am Benaiah!**
Narrator #1:	**Right.**
Benaiah:	**Mighty Man three!**
Narrator #1:	**That's right.**
Benaiah:	**Otherwise known as Arnold Schwarzenegger!**
Narrator #1:	**Oh, brother.**
Narrator #2:	**All three of them had great adventures!**
Eleazar:	*(Act out some karate moves)* **Hi-ya-ka-bung-ah!**
Ish-Bosheth:	*(Punch the air like a boxer)* **Take that! . . . and that . . . and a little of that!**
Benaiah:	*(Act out some professional wrestling moves)* **Body slam!**
Narrator #2:	**They were tough.**
Eleazar:	*(Flex muscles)*
Ish-Bosheth:	*(Flex muscles, make a mean face)*
Benaiah:	*(Poof your hair, then say)* **You toucha da hair, I breaka da face.**
Narrator #1:	**And they were great swordsmen.**
Eleazar:	*(Pretend to swordfight)* **On guard!**
Ish-Bosheth:	*(Pretend to swordfight)* **Tallyho!**
Benaiah:	*(Pretend to swordfight)* **Choppy, choppy!**

Narrator #2:	**And they were very brave. Three of them were such great warriors that they became known simply as "The Three." One of them was named Eleazar.**
Eleazar:	**That's me.**
Narrator #1:	**He once stood by David's side in a barley field when the rest of the Israelite army ran away.**
Eleazar:	**C'mon, Davey, baby! We can take these guys!**
Narrator #2:	**He fought so hard for so long that his hand stuck to his sword and he couldn't let go of it.**
Eleazar:	*(Make a fist and shake your arm)* **Um . . . who put the superglue on my sword?**
Narrator #2:	**It wasn't superglue. His muscles had squeezed the sword so long he couldn't let go!**
Eleazar:	**Whoa. I must be tough.**
Narrator #2:	**You are!**
Eleazar:	**All for one and one for all! . . .**
Mighty Men:	*(Together)* **YO!**
Narrator #1:	**And one day, he and his buddies broke through the enemy lines and snuck to a well just to get a cup of water for King David!**
Eleazar:	**We risked our lives for a cup of water?**
Narrator #1:	**Yup! You were very brave!**
Eleazar:	**Either that or we were very stupid. . . .**
Narrator #2:	**The leader of "The Three" was named Ish-Bosheth.**
Ish-Bosheth:	**That's me.**
Narrator #1:	**He once killed 800 men at one time using his spear.**
Ish-Bosheth:	**I named all my spears Britney.**

David's Mighty Men

Narrator #1:	**Why's that?**
Ish-Bosheth:	**So I could fight with Britney spears!**
Narrator #1:	**That was really bad.**
Ish-Bosheth:	**Thank you. . . . All for one and one for all! . . .**
Mighty Men:	*(Together)* **YO!**
Narrator #2:	**In addition to "The Three," David had a group of warriors known as "The Thirty." The most famous of them was a guy named Benaiah.**
Benaiah:	**That's me.**
Narrator #1:	**He killed off two of Moab's greatest warriors.**
Benaiah:	**Two for the price of one.**
Narrator #2:	**He once attacked a $7\frac{1}{2}$ foot tall Egyptian who had a spear.**
Benaiah:	**Was it named Britney?**
Narrator #2:	**No.**
Benaiah:	**Oh.**
Narrator #2:	**Benaiah had a club. He smacked the Egyptian, took the spear from his hands, and then killed him with his own spear! He was placed in charge of David's bodyguard.**
Benaiah:	**I must be brave.**
Narrator #1:	*(To Benaiah)* **You are.**
Benaiah:	**All for one and one for all! . . .**
Mighty Men:	*(Together)* **YO!**
Narrator #1:	**And once he followed a lion—**
Benaiah:	**—here kitty, kitty, kitty—**
Narrator #1:	**—into a pit—**
Benaiah:	**—that's the pits—**
Narrator #1:	**—on a snowy day.**

Benaiah:	**Wait a minute!**
Narrator #1:	**What?!**
Benaiah:	**I followed a lion—**
Narrator #1:	**Uh-huh.**
Benaiah:	**Into a pit?!**
Narrator #1:	**That's right.**
Benaiah:	**On a snowy day?!**
Narrator #1:	**Yup.**
Benaiah:	**I jumped into a pit with a lion in it?!**
Narrator #1:	**You sure did.**
Benaiah:	**In the middle of a snowstorm?!**
Narrator #1:	**Uh-huh.**
Benaiah:	**I must be very tough . . .**
Narrator #1:	**You are!**
Benaiah:	**. . . or crazy. . . .**
Narrator #2:	**All in all, those three men—**
Eleazar:	**Eleazar . . .**
Ish-Bosheth:	**Ish-Bosheth . . .**
Benaiah:	**And me, Arnold Schwarzenegger!**
Narrator #2:	**Um . . .**
Benaiah:	**OK . . . and me, Benaiah!**
Narrator #2:	**—were three of the greatest warriors and bravest fighters the world has ever seen.**
Mighty Men:	*(Together)* **All for one and one for all! . . . YO!**
Eleazar:	**We used our gifts . . .**
Ish-Bosheth:	**And our courage . . .**
Benaiah:	**And our stupidity!—**

Narrator #2:	*(Clear your throat)*
Benaiah:	—**I mean our strength . . .**
Eleazar:	**. . . to protect God's people . . .**
Ish-Bosheth:	**. . . to serve King David . . .**
Benaiah:	**. . . and to fight for truth, justice, and the American way! . . .**
Narrator #1:	*(Point to the audience)* **Whatever gifts God has given to you,**
Narrator #2:	**You can do the same.**
Mighty Men:	*(Together)* **All for one and one for all! . . . YO!**
Everyone:	*(Together)* **The end!**

(Smile, bow, and then take your seat.)

David's Mighty Men

SOLOMON'S RADICAL WISDOM

BASED ON: 1 Kings 3; 4:29-34 (see also 2 Chronicles 1:1-13)

BIG IDEA: When Solomon was faced with a difficult decision about the identity of a newborn baby, he showed that God had indeed given him great wisdom.

BACKGROUND: Before David died, he appointed Solomon to be the next king of Israel. Early in Solomon's reign, God asked him what gift he would like. Solomon chose a wise and discerning heart to govern the Israelites. (Note: Solomon didn't just ask for wisdom, but discernment in order to lead justly).

God was pleased with Solomon's choice and gave him even more than he asked for.

In this story, two women (who were both prostitutes) claim that a baby is theirs. Solomon orders that the baby be cut in half with a sword and, based on the reaction of the two women, discerns who the true mother was. As a result of this decision, news of Solomon's great wisdom spreads throughout the land.

NEW TESTAMENT CONNECTION: When Solomon was granted a unique opportunity to ask God for a special gift, he chose wisdom. God still grants wisdom to all believers who ask for it: "If any of you lacks wisdom, he should ask God, who gives generously to all without finding fault, and it will be given to him" (James 1:5).

CAST: You'll need 6-7 children for this QuickSkit: Narrator (girl or boy), Woman #1 (girl), Woman #2 (girl), Solomon (preferably a boy), Soldier (preferably a boy), Baby (preferably a boy), God (boy)

PROPS: A fake sword and a baby boy doll (optional)

TOPICS: Choices, giftedness, leadership, lying, prayer, success, wisdom

TIPS:
- You can use either a doll for the Baby, or you could use a real person. Woman #1 begins with the Baby. Give the sword to the Soldier.
- Position the Women next to each other on the left side of the stage. (If you use a live person as the Baby, then position that person next to the Women.) Place Solomon and the Soldier next to each other in the center, and the Narrator and God on the right side of the stage. Bring up the stage lights, and then begin when the listeners are quiet.

Director: Lights! . . . Camera! . . . Action!

Narrator: When Solomon became king, he had a special time of prayer. That night, God spoke to him.

God: Solomon, ask for anything you'd like and I'll give it to you!

Solomon: Hm, well . . . let's see. Leading all these people is a tough job. . . .

God: Yes, it is.

Solomon: So give me lots of wisdom, God, so I can tell right from wrong and make good decisions!

God: Good choice.

Solomon: Thank you.

God:	I'll also bless you with honor and riches because you made such a good choice.
Solomon:	Cool.
God:	And, if you keep my rules like your dad, King David, you'll get a nice, long life, too.
Solomon:	Well, thank you.
God:	You're welcome.
Narrator:	When Solomon woke up, he realized it had been a dream.
Solomon:	God spoke to me in a dream! Let's have a party and celebrate!
Narrator:	So Solomon worshiped God and threw a big party. Then one day some women came to Solomon with a problem.
Soldier:	Your majesty, there are two women here to see you.
Solomon:	Show them in.
Woman #1:	O King! We live together in the same house.
Solomon:	That's nice.
Woman #1:	Well, not long ago I had a baby. *(Hold up the Baby)*
Solomon:	Congratulations.
Woman #1:	Thank you. And a few days later, she had a baby, too.
Solomon:	Congratulations to you, too.
Woman #2:	Thank you.
Woman #1:	So we were all alone in the house one night. And while we were asleep, she rolled over and killed her baby.
Woman #2:	Did not! *(Take the Baby)*
Woman #1:	Did too! *(Take the Baby)*

Woman #2:	Did not! *(Take the Baby)*
Woman #1:	Did too!—*(Take the Baby)*
Solomon:	—Now, hold on there. Stop arguing. Finish your story.
Woman #1:	Well, during the night she switched the babies! *(Hand the Baby to Woman #2)* . . . She put the dead baby next to me, and she took my baby to keep for herself!
Woman #2:	Did not!
Woman #1:	Did too! *(Take the Baby)*
Woman #2:	Did not! *(Take the Baby)*
Woman #1:	Did too! *(Take the Baby)*
Solomon:	Stop it! What happened then?
Woman #1:	Well, when I woke up, I noticed that the baby next to me was dead! I thought it was mine, but when I looked closely, I realized it wasn't my baby at all! That's when I knew she'd switched 'em!
Woman #2:	Did not! *(Take the Baby)*
Woman #1:	Did too! *(Take the Baby)*
Woman #2:	Did not! *(Take the Baby)*
Woman #1:	Did too! *(Take the Baby)*
Woman #2:	SHE'S the one who switched 'em! *(Take the Baby)*
Woman #1:	Am not! *(Take the Baby)*
Woman #2:	Are too! *(Take the Baby)*
Woman #1:	Am not! *(Take the Baby)*
Woman #2:	Are too! *(Take the Baby)*
Woman #1:	No, no, NO! The DEAD baby is yours, and the LIVE one is mine! *(Take the Baby)*
Woman #2:	Is not! *(Take the Baby)*

Woman #1:	**Is too!** *(Take the Baby)*
Woman #2:	**Is not!** *(Take the Baby)*
Woman #1:	**Is too!** *(Take the Baby)*
Solomon:	**Quiet down, ladies!**
Soldier:	**You heard the king. Quiet down!** *(Raise your sword up and swing it around in the air)*
Woman #2:	*(Stick your tongue out at Woman #1)*
Woman #1:	*(Stick your tongue out at Woman #2)*
Solomon:	**Hm . . . they both claim the live baby is theirs and the dead one isn't. . . . Soldier?**
Soldier:	**Yes, your majesty?**
Solomon:	**Go get me a sword.**
Soldier:	*(Pick up the sword)* **Here you go, your majesty.**
Solomon:	**That was quick. . . .**
Soldier:	**Yes, of course, your majesty.**
Solomon:	**Alright. Take the sword and cut the baby in half. We'll give half of the baby to each woman.**
Soldier:	**As you wish, your majesty.** *(Take the Baby from the women)*

Narrator:	**When the baby's real mother heard that, she was afraid, for her heart was full of love for her child.**
Woman #1:	**No! Don't do it! Give the baby to her! Let it live!**
Woman #2:	**Go on; cut the baby in half. That way neither of us will have a baby.**
Soldier:	*(Raise the sword over the Baby)* **Should I really cut the baby in half, your majesty?**
Solomon:	**No! Don't hurt the baby. Give him to the first woman. She's the real mother. She wanted the baby to live no matter what. That's the kind of love that a mother has.**
Soldier:	**Yes, your majesty.** *(Hand the Baby to Woman #1)*
Woman #1:	*(Huge smiles, hug your Baby!)*
Woman #2:	*(Frown and pout)*
Narrator:	**When people heard what Solomon had said and done, they were amazed! They could tell God really had given him great wisdom. And news of Solomon's decision spread throughout the land.**
Everyone:	*(Together)* **The end!**

(Smile, bow, and then take your seat.)

THE KINGDOM IS TORN IN TWO

BASED ON: 1 Kings 11:9-13, 26-43; 1 Kings 12:1-24

BIG IDEA: Solomon's family lost power because he turned away from the Lord. As a result, Israel became a divided kingdom.

BACKGROUND: After David's rule, his son, Prince Solomon, became king of Israel. At first, King Solomon followed in the righteous footsteps of his father. But then, after marrying hundreds of unbelieving princesses (perhaps to shore up military alliances), he turned his heart toward idol worship.

God became angry with Solomon and told him he would lose his kingdom and Israel would become a divided nation. Then, when Solomon died, the split occurred just as God had said.

NEW TESTAMENT CONNECTION: We can learn from the consequences of Solomon's idolatry not to set our hearts on evil things as he did. This is one of the reasons we study stories from the Old Testament (see 1 Corinthians 10:6-11). We must worship the Lord and him alone: "Do not be idolaters, as some of them were" (1 Corinthians 10:7).

CAST: You'll need 4-6 children for this QuickSkit: Narrator (girl or boy), Elder (boy or girl), Buddy (preferably a boy), Ahijah (preferably a boy), Ray (preferably a boy), Jerry (preferably a boy)

PROPS: None

TOPICS: Advice, choices, consequences, leadership, stubbornness

TIPS:
- If you're short of students, you could perhaps use one person to read the parts of Ahijah, Elder, and Buddy.
- Position the Narrator and Ahijah next to each other on the left side of the stage, Ray and Jerry next to each other in the center, and Elder and Buddy on the right side of the stage. Bring up the stage lights, and then begin when the listeners are quiet.

Director: Lights! . . . Camera! . . . Action!

Narrator: Today's story is about King Solomon's son, Prince Rehoboam. We'll call him Ray for short.

Ray: That's me!

Narrator: And a leader named Jeroboam. We'll call him Jerry for short.

Jerry: That's me!

Narrator: Now you should know that God had sent a man named Ahijah to tell Jerry that he would be the next king.

Ahijah: You're gonna be the next king.

Jerry: Cool.

Ahijah: The 12 groups of people in Israel won't have one king anymore. Instead, they'll have two kings.

Jerry: How come?

Ahijah:	Well, Solomon has stopped worshipping God and has started to worship the idols of his many wives.
Jerry:	That's naughty.
Ahijah:	That's right; it is. Now, if you listen to God and obey him, your children and their children and their children's, children's children will keep ruling the land.
Jerry:	Cool.
Narrator:	But when Solomon heard about all that, he tried to have Jerry killed.
Jerry:	Yikes!
Narrator:	But Jerry escaped to Egypt.
Jerry:	Whew!
Narrator:	Finally, after Solomon died, Ray became the next king.
Ray:	Just call me King Ray!
Narrator:	But some of the people sent for Jerry because they knew he was a good leader.
Jerry:	That's very kind of you. Thank you. Thank you. Thank you.
Narrator:	They sent him to King Ray to ask him to be nice to them.
Jerry:	Hey, Stingray!
Ray:	That's King Ray.
Jerry:	Oh. Whatever.
Ray:	What do you want?
Jerry:	Be nice to us.
Ray:	Why should I do that?
Jerry:	Well, your dad was mean to us. He made us work too hard. But if you treat us kindly we'll be glad to serve you.

Ray:	Give me a couple of days to think about it.
Jerry:	OK, you've got three days.
Narrator:	And then Ray asked the men who'd advised his father, King Solomon, what he should do. . . .
Ray:	What should I do, old man?
Elder:	Be nice to the people! Then they'll always be on your side and be your friends! Serve them now, and then they'll serve you later!
Ray:	Hm . . . let me think about it.
Narrator:	But Ray also asked his buddies what to do. . . .
Ray:	What should I do, young cool dudes who are my age and my best friends in the whole wide world?
Buddy:	Tell the people, "If you thought my dad was mean, wait till I get going! You guys are toast!" Tell 'em that!
Ray:	Sounds good to me!
Narrator:	So Ray listened to the advice of his buddies . . .
Buddy:	Cool!
Narrator:	. . . Rather than the words of his father's advisers.
Elder:	You're gonna regret it!
Narrator:	Then Jerry and the people of the north came back for their answer.
Jerry:	OK, Stingray.
Ray:	That's King Ray.
Jerry:	Right. Whatever. You said to come back for an answer and here we are. What do you say, are you gonna be nice to us or not?

The Kingdom Is Torn in Two

Ray:	No way! If you thought my dad was mean, wait till I get going! You guys are toast!
Narrator:	Well, as you can imagine, they weren't too happy to hear that.
Jerry:	Forget you, man. We're outta here! C'mon, everybody! We'll set up our own kingdom north of here.
Ray:	You mean without King Ray?
Jerry:	Yeah, without King Ray. Or stingrays, or octopuses or anything.
Ray:	Oopsy.
Elder:	I told you so!
Narrator:	So the people stomped off and refused to listen to King Ray, and they made Jerry their king instead.
Jerry:	Just call me King Jerry.
Ray:	(Point to Buddy) Hey, make 'em come back!
Buddy:	OK. I will.
Narrator:	But the people killed the man King Ray sent after them.
Buddy:	Uh-oh. (Stick out your tongue and act dead)
Narrator:	And then they came after King Ray.
Ray:	Yikes.
Narrator:	They weren't too happy.
Ray:	I'm outta here!
Narrator:	So King Ray hopped onto his chariot and rode back to Jerusalem.
Ray:	Whew.
Elder:	I told you, you'd regret it, Mr. Stingray.
Ray:	That's King Ray! King Ray! I'm King Ray! I'm the king of the whole land!
Elder:	Not anymore.
Ray:	(Sadly) Oh yeah. Right.
Narrator:	And all this happened because God said it would.
Ahijah:	I told you so.
Narrator:	The country was split in half, and the kingdom of Solomon crumbled.
Elder:	I told him he'd regret it.
Narrator:	The northern kingdom became known as "Israel." And King Jerry ruled there.
Jerry:	That's me.
Narrator:	The southern kingdom became known as "Judah." And Stingray ruled there.
Ray:	You mean King Ray!
Narrator:	Oh, yeah. Whatever. . . . And the Kingdom of Israel was split in two because Solomon had sinned and turned his heart away from the Lord.
Everyone:	(Together) The end!

(Smile, bow, and then take your seat.)

The Kingdom Is Torn in Two

SHOWDOWN ON CARMEL MOUNTAIN

BASED ON: 1 Kings 17:1; 18:1-46

BIG IDEA: On Mt. Carmel, God proved that he was the one true God. Finally, the Israelites turned back to him.

BACKGROUND: Ahab and his family were wicked rulers in the northern kingdom (Israel). As a result, God's prophet Elijah prayed that God would not send rain or dew on the land. The Israelites were worshiping Baal, a god of fertility, but one believer's prayer showed how worthless this "god" was! During the drought, God protected and provided for Elijah in miraculous ways.

Finally, after more than three years, God told Elijah to set up a showdown where he would prove once and for all that he really was the Lord.

NEW TESTAMENT CONNECTION: Elijah stood up for the Lord even when it wasn't popular and when he was in the minority. Today, we are asked to the do same thing: "Therefore, since we have such a hope, we are very bold" (2 Corinthians 3:12).

CAST: You'll need 6-10 children for this QuickSkit: Narrator (girl or boy), 1-3 Baal Prophets (boys or girls), 1-3 Israelites (boys or girls), Obadiah (preferably a boy), Elijah (preferably a boy), King Ahab (preferably a boy)

PROPS: Two handfuls of raw hamburger, 12 cups of water, a bucket of water, a table, a towel (to clean up with), and a blowtorch (all optional)

TOPICS: Choices, conviction, courage, faith, God's existence, God's power, ministry (of the prophets), prayer, success, worship

TIPS:
- Make sure that you explain to all the children that the kids playing the part of the Baal Prophets aren't really praying to a false god, they're just saying their lines and pretending to be like the people long ago who didn't love the Lord. Help the audience and the readers understand that there's a difference between acting in a skit and doing something in real life.
- If you use props, have the handfuls of hamburger available for the Baal Prophets and Elijah. Place the 12 cups of water on the table next to the bucket of water. When the Israelites pour water on Elijah's altar, have them pour the water on the raw hamburger. When the part comes when God's fire burns it up, pull out the blow torch and wave it in front of the audience . . . (If you choose to do this, you'll need an adult to be the Narrator!)
- Position the Baal Prophets next to each other on the left side of the stage; the Israelites and the Narrator next to each other on the right side of the stage; and Obadiah, Elijah, and King Ahab in the center. Bring up the stage lights, and then begin when the listeners are quiet.

Director: **Lights! . . . Camera! . . . Action!**

Narrator: **Long ago, God's people began worshiping made-up gods, so Elijah prayed that no rain would fall on the land.**

Elijah: **God, make the rain go away and come again some other day!**

Narrator: **During that time the people of the land were very hot and thirsty.**

Israelites:	*(Together, stick out your tongue and pant like a thirsty dog)*
Narrator:	Dew didn't even fall on the grass at night!
Israelites:	*(Together)* We need some dew, dudes!
Narrator:	This went on for a long time . . .
Israelites:	*(Together, more panting)*
Narrator:	. . . until finally, in the third year, God told Elijah to go to King Ahab because he was ready to send rain on the land.
Elijah:	Whatever you say, God!
Narrator:	Now King Ahab had been looking for Elijah because he blamed him for the drought. He was also looking for water.
King Ahab:	Hey, Obadiah!
Obadiah:	Yes, your majesty?
King Ahab:	You're in charge of my palace, right?
Obadiah:	Of course, your majesty.
King Ahab:	Well, my royal pets are thirsty.
Obadiah:	Oh.
King Ahab:	Go through the country and look for some water to give them.
Obadiah:	OK.
King Ahab:	Look everywhere—lakes, streams, springs, and water towers.
Obadiah:	What's a water tower?
King Ahab:	I don't know, but it sounds like it might have some water.
Obadiah:	Oh. OK.
King Ahab:	Maybe between the two of us we'll find some water. You go that way. *(Point to the left)*
Obadiah:	Right.
King Ahab:	No, that's left.
Obadiah:	Right.
King Ahab:	And I'll go this way. *(Point to the right)*
Obadiah:	Right.
King Ahab:	That's right.
Obadiah:	Alright.
Narrator:	Now even though Obadiah worked for a wicked king, he loved the Lord. In fact, he had rescued 100 of God's prophets from a mean queen.
Obadiah:	I hid them in a cave! Hee, hee, hee, hee.
Narrator:	During his trip to find water, he found something else—he found Elijah.
Obadiah:	Whoa! Is it really you?
Elijah:	Yup, it's me. Now, go back to King Ahab and tell him I wanna talk to him.
Narrator:	So Obadiah went and set up the meeting.
King Ahab:	So, Elijah! There you are, you troublemaker!
Elijah:	I'm not the troublemaker; you are! You and your family brought trouble on everyone because you turned away from the Lord!
Narrator:	Ahab and his family had started worshiping made-up gods. One was called "Baal" and the other one was called "Asherah." Their idol worship caused many people to turn away from God. That made God very angry.
Elijah:	Now call everyone in the country together at Mount Carmel. We'll have a showdown to see who the real God is!
King Ahab:	Sounds good to me.
Elijah:	Oh yeah, and bring all 450 prophets of Baal and 400 prophets of Asherah.

Showdown on Carmel Mountain

King Ahab:	You've got a deal.
Narrator:	So Ahab called everyone together at Mount Carmel. Then Elijah spoke to the people of Israel:
Elijah:	How long are you gonna put off choosing who to serve? Huh? If the Lord is God, serve him. If Baal is God, serve him. Quit going back and forth from one to the other!
Narrator:	But the people didn't say anything. They just stood there.
Israelites:	Duh . . .
Elijah:	OK. Get two bulls. We'll take turns. We'll cut 'em up and lay the meat on some wood. Then the prophets of Baal—
Baal Prophets:	*(Together)*—that's us!—
Elijah:	—yeah, well, you can call out to your gods. I'll call on the Lord, and we'll see who sends fire. Whichever one does is the real God.
Israelites:	Groovy.
Narrator:	So the prophets of Baal took a bull, cut it up, and laid it on the wood.
Baal Prophets:	*(Together, take a handful of the raw hamburger and slap it on the table in front of you)*
Narrator:	Then, all morning, they asked Baal to send fire. . . .
Baal Prophets:	*(Together, imitating cheerleaders)* Baal! Baal! Burn our meat! Send some fire! Send some heat! Burn this bull and show you're real! C'mon, Baal! Cook our meal!
Narrator:	But of course, no fire came. Because their god was just made-up.
Baal Prophets:	Baal! Baal! What's the deal? Cook us up some roasted veal!
Narrator:	By noon, Elijah had started to make fun of them.
Elijah:	Yell louder! Maybe your god fell asleep! Or maybe he's going to the bathroom, or on vacation or something. Maybe he's taking a nap! Go on; see if you can wake him up.
Baal Prophets:	*(Imitating cheerleaders, louder this time)* BAAL! BAAL! BURN OUR MEAT! SEND SOME FIRE! SEND SOME HEAT! BURN THIS BULL AND SHOW YOU'RE REAL! C'MON, BAAL! COOK OUR MEAL!
Narrator:	Then the prophets got all crazy about it. They danced around screaming and carrying on . . . until finally, that evening, Elijah said to the people,
Elijah:	OK, everyone. It's my turn.
Israelites:	Groovy.
Narrator:	He piled up 12 rocks, laid some wood on top, and then dug a ditch around the pile. Then he cut up the bull and laid the meat on the wood.
Elijah:	*(Take a handful of the raw hamburger and slap it on the table in front of you)* OK. Now fill up four big jars of water and pour it on the meat.
Israelites:	OK. *(Pour 3 cups of water on Elijah's hamburger)*
Elijah:	Do it again.
Israelites:	You asked for it! *(Pour 3 more cups of water on Elijah's hamburger)*
Elijah:	And again.
Israelites:	Whatever you say! *(Pour 3 more cups of water on Elijah's hamburger)*
Narrator:	The wood and the meat *(and the table . . .)* were soaked. And water had filled the ditch around it all, too.
Israelites:	Groovy. Gravy.

Elijah:	*(Praying)* **Lord, show these people here today that this whole thing was your idea. Prove that you're real so the people will turn back to you!**
Narrator:	**Suddenly, fire fell from heaven.** *(Hold up the blowtorch, let the kids see it, then say, "Just kidding!")*
Israelites:	**Whoa. Very groovy.**
Narrator:	**God burned up the meat, the wood, the rocks and even the dirt and water.** *(Sweep Elijah's hamburger off the table with your hand)*
Baal Prophets:	**Whoa.**
Israelites:	**The Lord is God! The Lord is real! So we will bow! And we will kneel! We'll worship him and him alone! We'll make those bad guys scream and moan!**
Narrator:	**Then Elijah had the false prophets rounded up . . .**
Baal Prophets:	**Uh-oh.**
Narrator:	**. . . arrested . . .**
Baal Prophets:	**Yikes.**
Narrator:	**. . . and killed off. . . .**
Baal Prophets:	**Ouch!** *(Stick out your tongue, tilt your head and look dead)*
Narrator:	**Then Elijah prayed for rain, and before long, the clouds were forming, the wind was blowing, and the rain was falling at last.** *(Pick up the bucket of water and splash it in the face of the Israelites)*
Israelites:	**Groovy.**
Elijah:	**Get out of here, King Ahab, or you're gonna get stuck in the mud!**
King Ahab:	**OK, okay, I believe you now, Elijah! Whatever you say!**
Narrator:	**And everyone knew that the Lord is the only God. And that he really IS in control.**
Everyone:	*(Together)* **The end!**

(Smile, bow, and then take your seat.)

Showdown on Carmel Mountain

THE SIEGE OF SAMARIA

BASED ON: 2 Kings 6:24–7:20

BIG IDEA: God frightened the army of Aram away from the city of Samaria, fulfilling Elisha's prophecy and delivering his people from the siege of the Arameans.

BACKGROUND: After Elijah the prophet was taken up into heaven, God spoke through his student, Elisha. The sins of the northern tribes (which became known as Israel) became worse and worse. Their nemesis became the country of Aram and, in about 850 b.c., the Arameans surrounded the capital city of Samaria and laid siege to it.

The people were so desperate that they even turned to cannibalism. God miraculously drove the army away, but only after making it abundantly clear to Samaria's faithless King Joram that the Lord was still in control.

NEW TESTAMENT CONNECTION: Just like the lepers in this story who had good news that they were tempted to keep to themselves, we have the best news of all! We can let people who are trapped in sin know that the siege is over, God has destroyed our enemy, and they can leave their old life and have all the blessings he offers: "I am not ashamed of the gospel, because it is the power of God for the salvation of everyone who believes" (Romans 1:16).

CAST: You'll need 6-8 children for this QuickSkit: Narrator #1 (girl or boy), Narrator #2 (girl or boy), Leper #1 (boy or girl), Leper #2 (boy or girl), Woman (girl), King Joram (preferably a boy), Elijah (preferably a boy), King's Aide (preferably a boy)

PROPS: None

TOPICS: Cannibalism, consequences, doubt, fear, God's sovereignty, hope, ministry (of the prophets), prophecy fulfillment, suffering

TIPS:
- If you have only six readers, Narrator #1 can also read Leper #1's part, and Narrator #2 can read Leper #2's part in addition to her own.
- Position the Narrators next to each other, the Lepers next to each other, King Joram and the King's Aide next to each other, and Elisha and the Woman next to each other. Bring up the stage lights, and then begin when the listeners are quiet.
- Note: Because of its graphic content, use discernment when performing this story for younger students.

Director: Lights! . . . Camera! . . . Action!

Narrator #1: After the country of Israel was split in two, the city of Samaria became the capital of the northern kingdom.

Narrator #2: One day, Ben-Hadad, the king of Aram, surrounded the city with his army and wouldn't let anyone get in or out.

Woman: We're hungry! We're thirsty! And we wanna get out! We're hungry! We're thirsty! And we wanna get out!

Narrator #2: And the people were saying stuff like, "I'm hungry enough to eat a horse."

Woman: I'm hungry enough to eat a horse!

Narrator #1: Actually, a donkey.

Narrator #2:	**Huh?**
Narrator #1:	**They were hungry enough to eat donkeys.**
Narrator #2:	**Really?**
Narrator #1:	**Yup, and, um . . . dove's dung.**
Narrator #2:	**Bird poop?!**
Narrator #1:	**Yup.**
Narrator #2:	**They ate bird poop?!**
Narrator #1:	**Yeah.**
Narrator #2:	**That's disgusting!**
Narrator #1:	**Well, the people were starving to death and had to eat something. . . .**
Woman:	**We're hungry! We're thirsty! And we wanna get out! We're hungry! We're thirsty! And we wanna get out!**
Narrator #2:	**So one day the king of Samaria was walking along the top of the city walls, when a woman called to him.**
Woman:	**O King! Save me!**
King Joram:	*(Angrily)* **If God won't save you, what do you expect me to do?** *(Sighing)* **What's the problem?**
Woman:	**A woman told me to bring her my son so we could eat him. So we did.**
King Joram:	**What?!**
Woman:	**And she promised we could eat her baby the next day.**
King Joram:	**You can't be serious!**
Woman:	**I am and we did. We boiled my son and ate him.**
King Joram:	**Oh, no!**
Woman:	**But the next day she'd hidden her son. O King! Make her give me her son so I can have him for supper!**

Narrator #1:	**That's the most terrible thing I've ever heard!**
Narrator #2:	**It was the most terrible thing the king had ever heard, too. He was filled with grief and anger.**
King Joram:	*(Angrily)* **Oh! I'll get Elisha for this! It's all his fault! He's a dead man!**
Narrator #1:	**The king blamed God's prophet Elisha for all the problems. So he sent some men to kill him!**
Narrator #2:	**Now Elisha was at home, and God told him men were coming from the king.**
Elisha:	**Shut the door and hold it shut! Those men were sent to kill me!**
King Joram:	*(To Elisha)* **Elisha, the Lord has done this to us! Why should I sit around here any longer waiting for God to help us? He doesn't care about us anymore!**
Elisha:	**This is what God says, "By this time tomorrow, you'll have loads and loads of food! It'll be cheap to buy!"**
Narrator #2:	**Now the man helping the king laughed at that.**
King's Aide:	**Yeah, right. Even if God would open up a trapdoor in heaven and pour out food on top of our heads, that would never happen!**
Elisha:	**Oh, it'll happen alright. And you'll see it, but you won't eat any of it.**
King's Aide:	**Whatever.**
Elisha:	**Trust me.**
King's Aide:	**Whatever.**
Narrator #1:	**Meanwhile, there were four men living outside the city walls by themselves.**
Narrator #2:	**They had a disease called leprosy that made their skin die, and nobody wanted to be near them.**

The Siege of Samaria

Leper #1:	Hey, listen. We're starving out here, right?
Leper #2:	Right.
Leper #1:	And if we go into the city, we'll just starve in there, too, right?
Leper #2:	Right. So?
Leper #1:	So let's surrender to the army of Aram. Who knows? They might kill us—
Leper #2:	—they sure might—
Leper #1:	—but they might not. They might let us live, so what have we got to lose?
Leper #2:	Good point.
Narrator #1:	So, at twilight, the four men with leprosy headed to the camp of the enemy. But when they got there, it was empty.
Leper #2:	Hello?
Leper #1:	Is anybody there?
Narrator #2:	God had made the army of Aram hear another army charging toward them.
Narrator #1:	And they got scared because they thought it was the Egyptians or the Hittites. They totally freaked out.
Narrator #2:	Let's get outta here!
Narrator #1:	And they left everything behind 'em—food, tents, horses, donkeys, money, even their clothes.
Narrator #2:	Ah! Yikes! *(Cross your arms in front of you like you're covering your nakedness)*
Leper #1:	Look at all this stuff! It's all ours now!
Leper #2:	Good point! And look, food!
Leper #1:	Chow time!

Narrator #2:	So they ate their fill, and then they put on some new clothes and filled the pockets with gold and silver. Then, they hid some of the treasure in the sand and went back for more.
Leper #1:	Um . . . you know what?
Leper #2:	What?
Leper #1:	What we're doing isn't right. . . .
Leper #2:	What do you mean?
Leper #1:	Well, this is a day of good news and we're keeping it to ourselves.
Leper #2:	Hm. Good point.
Leper #1:	C'mon, let's tell the people in the city!
Narrator #2:	So they went back and called to the guard by the gate,
Leper #1:	Hey! The enemy is gone! There's food for everyone. And gold and silver and horses!
Leper #2:	And play dough and Barbie dolls!
Leper #1:	There isn't any play dough and Barbie dolls!
Leper #2:	Oh. Too bad.
Leper #1:	But there are clothes and weapons!
Narrator #1:	So the guard went and told the king what the lepers had told him.
King Joram:	Hm . . . it's probably a trap. Our enemies want us to leave the city, and then they'll jump out of the shadows and attack us!
King's Aide:	How about we send a couple of men to check it out?
King Joram:	Good idea. Round up some horses and a few brave men to see if it's true.

The Siege of Samaria

Narrator #2:	So a couple of soldiers headed out and found that everything the lepers said was true.
Narrator #1:	All along the road they found weapons, equipment, and clothes—
Narrator #2:	Ah! Yikes! *(Cross your arms in front of you like you're covering your nakedness)*
Narrator #1:	—that the Aramean army had left behind when they ran away.
King's Aide:	It's true, O King! God must have scared 'em out of their pants!
Narrator #2:	Ah! Yikes! *(Cross your arms in front of you like you're covering your nakedness)*
King Joram:	Hm . . . I guess he did.
King's Aide:	It's not a trap after all! Open the gates. It's suppertime!
King Joram:	Chow time!
Narrator #2:	So the king's helper opened the city doors and all those hungry people ran out.
King Joram:	Watch out! Here they come!
Narrator #1:	But the king's helper couldn't get out of the way in time.

King's Aide:	Uh-oh.
Narrator #2:	And the hungry people ran him over.
King's Aide:	Ouch.
Narrator #1:	And killed him on the spot.
King's Aide:	I want my mommy. . . .
King Joram:	Nasty.
Narrator #2:	It all happened just like Elisha the Prophet had predicted. Everything came true just like he'd said.
Narrator #1:	God was in control the whole time.
Leper #1:	*(After a pause)* Sometimes God lets good things happen to bless his people . . .
Leper #2:	That's a good point.
Leper #1:	. . . and sometimes he lets bad things happen so his people will turn back to him.
Leper #2:	That's a good point, too.
Everyone:	*(Together)* The end!

(Smile, bow, and then take your seat.)

The Siege of Samaria

JOASH RESTORES THE TEMPLE

BASED ON: 2 Chronicles 24; 2 Kings 12

BIG IDEA: The young King Joash spearheaded a campaign to refurbish God's temple. After he overcame some setbacks, the temple was finally restored.

BACKGROUND: God's temple had fallen into disuse and neglect. When the young boy, Joash, became king of Judah (the southern kingdom) at age seven, he began a series of steps to restore God's temple.

As long as the priest Jehoiada was alive, Joash followed God. But late in his reign he began to let evil influences lead him away from the Lord. He actually ended up murdering his old mentor's son and dying a painful and disgraceful death himself.

Don't confuse this story with the reforms of another young king, named Josiah. He was 8 years old when he became king and led a much more exhaustive spiritual reformation in Judah.

NEW TESTAMENT CONNECTION: Passing on your faith from generation to generation is a theme of this story and is woven throughout the New Testament (see 2 Timothy 1:5). The idea, though, is to remain faithful to God, even when our spiritual mentors are no longer with us: "It is fine to be zealous, provided the purpose is good, and to be so always and not just when I am with you" (Galatians 4:18).

CAST: You'll need 3-4 children for this QuickSkit: Narrator (girl or boy), Sign Holder (girl or boy), Jehoiada (preferably a boy), Joash (preferably a boy)

PROPS: Three signs: One that reads, "Hooray!"; another that reads, "Boo!"; and a third that reads, "Listen up, everybody!"

TOPICS: Consequences, faithfulness, following God, leadership, mentors, obedience, worship

TIPS:
- Be sure that your Narrator knows how to pronounce "Jehoiada."
- The Sign Holder doesn't have any lines. All he (or she) does is hold up the signs at the appropriate times. If you don't have enough children, you could have the Narrator also serve as the Sign Holder.
- Position the Narrator and the Sign Holder next to each other on stage, and Jehoiada and Joash next to each other on stage. Bring up the stage lights, and then begin when the listeners are quiet.

Director: **Lights! . . . Camera! . . . Action!**

Narrator: *(To the audience)* **For today's story, we're gonna need your help! We have three signs that we'll hold up during the story. Whenever we hold up a sign, read it really loudly. The first sign is when something good happens. . . .**

Sign Holder: *(Hold up the "Hooray!" sign, let the audience respond, then set it down)*

Narrator: **Good. The second sign is when something bad happens. . . .**

Sign Holder: *(Hold up the "Boo!" sign, let the audience respond, then set it down)*

Narrator: **And the third sign is for the king's teacher. . . .**

Sign Holder:	*(Hold up the "Listen up, everybody!" sign, let the audience respond, then set it down)*
Narrator:	**Great. Now, let's get started. . . .**
Sign Holder:	*("Listen up, everybody!")*
Narrator:	**Joash was 7 years old when he became the king. . . .**
Sign Holder:	*("Hooray!")*
Joash:	**Now that I'm king, I'd like to make a new law. From now on, it's against the law to give out homework!**
Sign Holder:	*("Hooray!")*
Narrator:	**Um . . . he didn't quite say that. But he did invite over his teacher, a priest named Jehoiada. . . .**
Sign Holder:	*("Listen up, everybody!")*
Joash:	**Let's fix up the temple!**
Jehoiada:	**How?**
Joash:	**We'll ask people for money and give it to the priests, and they can fix anything that's broken.**
Jehoiada:	**That's pretty trusting.**
Joash:	**If you can't trust a priest, who can you trust?**
Jehoiada:	**Good point.**
Joash:	**And do it right away! Go through the land and ask people for money to fix up God's temple.**
Jehoiada:	**OK! I'll tell the other priests!**
Sign Holder:	*("Hooray!")*
Narrator:	**But the priests didn't fix the temple. Year after year they did nothing. They were lazy!**
Sign Holder:	*("Boo!")*
Joash:	**Why aren't you fixing the temple?**

Jehoiada:	**I don't know. I guess the other priests are just too lazy. . . .**
Sign Holder:	*("Boo!")*
Joash:	**Well, they're not getting any more money, that's for sure. They didn't do the work!**
Sign Holder:	*("Boo!")*
Joash:	**Let's hire some men who are good at fixing up stuff—carpenters and masons and people like that.**
Sign Holder:	*("Hooray!")*
Narrator:	**So they did. Until one day, Jehoiada came to talk to Joash. As you remember, he was Joash's teacher. . . .**
Sign Holder:	*("Listen up, everybody!")*
Jehoiada:	**I have an idea, your majesty.**
Joash:	**What's that?**
Jehoiada:	**How about I put a box by the altar, and then when people come to worship they can drop money in it?**
Joash:	**You wanna take an offering?**
Jehoiada:	**Um . . . yeah. Something like that.**
Joash:	**OK. That way those lazy priests . . .**
Sign Holder:	*("Boo!")*
Joash:	**Won't waste any more of our money.**
Sign Holder:	*("Hooray!")*
Jehoiada:	**Right. And then we can pay the stonecutters and carpenters and the smiths and other workers.**
Sign Holder:	*("Hooray!")*
Joash:	**Right. And we won't use that money for extra stuff like bowls, trumpets, knives or anything. Just the repairs.**
Jehoiada:	**Right!**

Joash Restores the Temple

Sign Holder:	*("Hooray!")*
Joash:	**Great!**
Jehoiada:	**Hey, you could write a song about this! . . . If I had a hammer . . . I'd hammer in the te-e-emple—**
Joash:	**—What are you talking about?**
Jehoiada:	**Never mind. It must be before your time.**
Joash:	**Oh.**
Sign Holder:	*("Hooray!")*
Joash:	**OK. Choose people you can trust—really trust—to be in charge—**
Jehoiada:	**OK.**
Joash:	**—and make it so.**
Jehoiada:	**Aye, aye. Captain.**
Narrator:	**And so, Jehoiada, the teacher . . .**
Sign Holder:	*("Listen up, everybody!")*
Narrator:	**. . . did what the king ordered. And when the repairs were all done, there was extra money left over.**
Jehoiada:	**Um, Joash?**
Joash:	**Yes?**
Jehoiada:	**We finished up the repairs and we have some money left. Should we buy that extra stuff now?**
Joash:	**Sure!**
Sign Holder:	*("Hooray!")*
Narrator:	**And so the work was completed because King Joash listened to his teacher, Jehoiada. . . .**
Sign Holder:	*("Listen up, everybody!")*

Narrator:	**But when Jehoiada died, Joash turned from the Lord.**
Sign Holder:	*("Boo!")*
Narrator:	**He worshiped made-up gods . . .**
Sign Holder:	*("Boo!")*
Narrator:	**And led people away from the Lord . . .**
Sign Holder:	*("Boo!")*
Joash:	**Oops.**
Jehoiada:	**That was naughty.**
Joash:	**I know. I blew it.**
Narrator:	**And so the moral of the story is that you should listen to your teachers . . .**
Sign Holder:	*("Listen up, everybody!")*
Narrator:	**When they teach you about God . . .**
Sign Holder:	*("Hooray!")*
Joash:	**Just like Joash did when he was a kid . . .**
Sign Holder:	*("Hooray!")*
Jehoiada:	**Before he turned away from God as a grown-up . . .**
Sign Holder:	*("Boo!")*
Narrator:	**Because God doesn't want your love for just a little while; he deserves your love for ALL of your life!**
Sign Holder:	*("Hooray!")*
Everyone:	*(Together)* **The end!**

(Smile, bow, and then take your seat.)

JONAH AND THE BASKING SHARK

BASED ON:	Jonah 1–4
BIG IDEA:	Jonah's prejudice against the people of Nineveh caused him to resent God's compassion toward them.
BACKGROUND:	Assyria was an enemy of Israel and was famous in the ancient world for its cruelty. When God called Jonah to preach repentance to them (Nineveh was their capital city), he wanted nothing to do with obeying God. He feared God just might turn their hearts around, and Jonah didn't want the Assyrians to receive God's mercy (see Jonah 4:2).
	The book of Jonah ends before we find out if Jonah ever repented of his prejudice.
	God's message is for all people and his grace is without bounds. When God wants to show compassion to someone, who are we to judge him?
NEW TESTAMENT CONNECTION:	Jesus' story of the workers hired throughout the day to work in the vineyard (Matthew 20:1-16) and his story of the lost son (Luke 15:11-32) have similar themes to the story of Jonah (i.e. resentment over God's grace on those we don't think are worthy of it).
	Also, Jesus referred to the story of Jonah as an illustration of his own death and resurrection (see Matthew 12:38-42).
CAST:	You'll need 4-5 children for this QuickSkit: Narrator #1 (girl or boy), Narrator #2 (girl or boy), Sailor #1 (girl or boy), Sailor #2/Jonah (preferably a boy)
PROPS:	Baseball caps and baggy jackets for the readers (optional)
TOPICS:	Basking sharks, calling, compassion, consequences, following God, God's love, God's sovereignty, grace, hiding, listening to God, ministry (of the prophets), obedience, prejudice, rebellion, second chances, stubbornness, witnessing
TIPS:	• Since this script is so word-intensive and has a specific rhythm, you'll want to have the readers practice before presenting it to the other students. If you chose to present it as a rap song, give your readers colorful costumes to wear!
	• To help the readers keep track of the words that are meant to rhyme with each other and the overall rhythmic patterns, rhyming words appear in all capital letters. You may wish to demonstrate how to emphasize words that rhyme when reading aloud.
	• Position the Narrators next to each other, and the Sailors and Jonah next to each other. (If you use four readers, have Sailor #2 also read the lines for Jonah.) Bring up the stage lights, and then begin when the listeners are quiet.

Director: **Lights! . . . Camera! . . . Action!**

Everyone: *(Together)* **Jonah was a prophet. He was brave and TRUE; But one day he didn't do what God wanted him TO.**

Sailors: *(Together)* **He tried to run away On a ship for Tar-SHISH;**

Narrators #1 & #2: *(Together)* **But the Lord sent a storm And he sent a giant FISH . . . Boyz!**

Narrator #1:	'Cause, God told Jonah, Go to NINEVEH! Tell 'em all to repent of their SINS AND THE . . . bad things they DO. 'Cause they haven't got a CLUE! Go, Jonah, go! I'm talking to YOU!
Everyone:	*(Together)* Go, Jonah! . . . Go, Jonah! . . . Go, go, go!
Narrator #2:	But Jonah ran away on a ship that DAY.
Narrator #1:	No, he didn't . . .
Narrator #2:	No, he didn't . . .
Narrator #1:	No, he didn't OBEY.
Narrator #2:	Soon a storm came blowin' in over the SEA.
Narrator #1:	Like a hurricane—
Narrator #2:	Or a TSUNAMI.
Narrator #1:	All the sailors got scared. . . . *(Pause)*
Sailors:	*(Act really scared)*
Narrator #2:	They were freaked and AFRAID. . . .
Sailors:	*(Act even more scared)*
Narrator #1:	They shouted,
Sailors:	*(Together)* Pray to your gods!
Narrator #1:	And they bowed. And they PRAYED. . . .
Narrator #2:	But their gods didn't help 'cause their gods were PRETEND,
Narrator #1:	And they all thought their lives were comin' to an END.
Everyone:	*(Together)* We're dead! . . . We're dead! . . . We're dead, dead meat!
Narrator #1:	The men dumped cargo from their ship to the SEA,
Narrator #2:	And the captain found Jonah on his bed ASLEEP.
Everyone:	*(Together)* Snore! . . . Snore! . . . Snore, snore, snore!

Sailor #1:	Wake up! We're afraid! And we've lost our NERVE, So, c'mon! Say a prayer to the God that you SERVE!
Narrator #2:	But Jonah didn't pray 'cause he already KNEW Why the Lord was mad and why the hurricane BLEW. Because . . .
Everyone:	*(Together)* Jonah was a prophet. He was brave and TRUE; But one day he didn't do what God wanted him TO. He tried to run away On a ship for Tar-SHISH; But the Lord sent a storm And he sent a giant FISH . . . Boyz!
Sailor #1:	Where do you live, man? What do you DO? And why would God send a big storm to get YOU?
Jonah:	I'm runnin' AWAY. I didn't OBEY! And now I know God's not happy TODAY!
Everyone else:	*(Together, looking at Jonah)* NO KIDDING, DUDE!
Narrator #2:	*(Sing to the tune of the "Gilligan's Isle" theme song)* The weather started getting rough; The tiny ship was tossed. If not for the courage of the fearless crew—
Everyone else:	*(Together)*—Wrong! . . . Wrong! . . . Wrong, wrong song!
Narrator #2:	Oh . . .
Jonah:	It's all my fault. I disobeyed the LORD. Now save yourselves! Throw me OVERBOARD!
Narrator #1:	The sailors tried hard to row the boat to SHORE,
Narrator #2:	But the wind blew harder than it had BEFORE!

Jonah and the Basking Shark

Narrator #1:	So they tossed our hero off into the SEA.
Narrator #2:	And a shark ate him up as a tasty TREAT.
Narrator #1:	Wait a minute! Wasn't it a whale?
Narrator #2:	Well, the Bible says it was a fish.
Narrator #1:	Yeah, so?
Narrator #2:	Whales are mammals, not fish. The only fish large enough to swallow a man is a shark.
Narrator #1:	A shark?!
Narrator #2:	Yeah. Probably a basking shark. They have huge mouths and tiny teeth, so Jonah could have easily survived. And they grow up to 33 feet long.
Narrator #1:	Whoa.
Everyone:	*(Together)* Gulp! . . . Gulp! . . . Gulp, gulp, gulp!
Narrator #2:	Then the storm stopped BLOWIN'! And the waves stopped FLOWIN'!
Narrator #1:	So the sailors started SHOWIN' Their thanks to God . . .
Everyone:	*(Together)* Pray! . . . Pray! . . . Pray, pray, pray!
Narrator #2:	*(After a pause)* And then . . . Jonah spent three days in the belly of the shark.
Everyone:	*(Together)* Dark! . . . Dark! . . . Dark, dark, dark!
Narrator #1:	Now spending three days in the belly of a FISH
Narrator #2:	Is enough to make anyone do the Lord's WISH.
Narrator #1:	Then the fish spit him up near the Nineveh SHORE,
Narrator #2:	And he got another message from his mighty LORD,

Narrator #1:	"Jonah! Go and preach all the words I SAID! If they don't repent, then they'll all be DEAD!"
Narrator #2:	So Jonah walked up smelling just like BILE
Narrator #1:	From the stomach,
Narrator #2:	Of the shark,
Narrator #1:	Where he'd been for AWHILE!
Everyone:	*(Together)* Yuck! . . . Yuck! . . . Yuck, yuck, yuck!
Jonah:	Forty days, that's all! Forty days, that's IT! Just forty short days is the time you GET! If you don't believe, you'll all be DEAD. So you better repent like God has SAID!
Narrator #2:	Well, the people heard that, and I know it's ODD,
Narrator #1:	But Jonah's little sermon turned 'em all to GOD.
Narrator #2:	They changed their minds. They changed their WAYS,
Narrator #1:	And they all lived past those forty DAYS.
Narrator #2:	They said they were sorry. And they said they were BAD.
Narrator #1:	And they cried and they prayed and they felt really SAD.
Everyone:	*(Together)* Waa! . . . Waa! . . . Waa, waa, waa!
Narrator #2:	When God saw the change, he forgave 'em ALL.
Narrator #1:	They believed.
Narrator #2:	They were saved.
Narrator #1:	And they had a BALL.
Narrator #2:	But Jonah still hadn't changed his MIND.
Narrator #1:	He hated those people.
Narrator #2:	He complained and WHINED.

Jonah and the Basking Shark

Narrator #1:	But God asked Jonah,
Narrator #2:	Why be mad at ME? I love 'em, like I loved you in the depths of the SEA.
Sailor #1:	For our God is great.
Sailor #2:	And his love is GRAND.
Sailor #1:	And it's meant for all people of every LAND.
Sailor #2:	So don't be whiny and make a FUSS.
Sailor #1:	Just be thankful he gave his love to US!
Everyone:	*(Together)* Yeah! . . . Yeah! . . . Yeah, yeah, yeah!
Sailor #2:	I said don't be whiny and make a—
Sailors:	*(Together)*—FUSS!
Sailor #1:	Just be thankful he gave his love to—
Sailors:	*(Together)*—US!
Everyone:	*(Together)* The end! . . . End! . . . End, end, end!

(Smile, bow, and then take your seat.)

Jonah and the Basking Shark

WHOLEHEARTED HEZEKIAH

BASED ON: 2 Kings 18:1-16; 20:1-21; Isaiah 38–39; 2 Chronicles 29–31; 32:24-33

BIG IDEA: King Hezekiah is one of the few people in the Bible whom we're told followed the Lord wholeheartedly. As far as kings go, he was second only to King David in his devotion and dedication to God.

BACKGROUND: After Hezekiah became king of Judah (the southern kingdom), he instituted a series of religious reforms, including cleaning and rededicating the temple and calling the country to repentance.

At one point, he was miraculously healed by God, but then naively showed off his treasures to the Babylonian envoys.

Every prayer of Hezekiah's that's recorded in Scripture was answered by God. Even though he struggled with pride for awhile after he was healed by God, he humbled himself again. Through it all, Hezekiah remained faithful to God.

NEW TESTAMENT CONNECTION: At the beginning of his reign, Hezekiah had the people (1) find what didn't belong in God's temple, (2) get rid of it, (3) ask for forgiveness, and then (4) commit to following God. Believers today are God's temple (1 Corinthians 3:16). We need to go through the same process, not with a building, but with our own hearts (see Ephesians 4:22-24).

CAST: You'll need 4-5 children for this QuickSkit: Narrator (girl or boy, for act #2), Narrator #1 (girl or boy, for act #1), Narrator #2 (girl or boy, for act #1), Hezekiah (preferably a boy, for act #2), Isaiah (preferably a boy, for act #2)

PROPS: Two signs for act #1. One that reads, "Boys!" another that reads, "Girls!"

TOPICS: Astronomical anomalies, following God, integrity, leadership, obedience, prayer, pride, priorities, repentance, worship

TIPS:
- This script is divided into two short acts that cover different aspects of Hezekiah's reign.
- The first act is a rap you can perform with your class. You'll only need two readers for this act. To help the readers keep track of the words that rhyme with each other and the overall rhythmic patterns, rhyming words appear in all capital letters.
- The second act is a conversation between Isaiah and Hezekiah. You'll also need a Narrator for this act (it could be the same person as Narrator #1).
- Position the readers as desired on stage. Bring up the stage lights, and then begin when the listeners are quiet.

(ACT 1 – HEZEKIAH CLEANS GOD'S TEMPLE)

Director: **Lights! . . . Camera! . . . Action!**

Narrator #1: **When Hezekiah became king, he took out the altars to the false gods.**

Narrator #2: **He smashed the idol stones and even the bronze snake Moses had made, because the people had started to worship it.**

Narrator #1:	He told people to clean out God's temple. When they were done, they all had a big party to celebrate God's goodness!
Narrator #2:	We're gonna do a little rap to tell the story of these changes Hezekiah made. And YOU get to help us with the words!
Narrator #1:	The boys' part goes, "He followed the Lord! He followed the Lord!" Let's practice. . . . *(Hold up the "Boys!" sign and let them respond . . .)*
Narrator #2:	Good. The girls' part goes, "Hezekiah was a guy who followed the Lord!" Let's try that . . . *(Hold up the "Girls!" sign and let them respond . . .)* **Great! Let's get started. . . . And let's see who can be louder, the boys or the girls!**
Narrator #1: Boys:	*(Hold up the "Boys!" sign)* He followed the Lord! He followed the Lord!
Narrator #2: Girls:	*(Hold up the "Girls!" sign)* Hezekiah was a guy who followed the Lord!

(Repeat the chorus again)

Narrator #1:	On the very first day that he was made KING,
Narrator #2:	Hezekiah did a very unexpected THING.
Narrator #1:	He opened up the temple and invited people IN,
Narrator #2:	And he said, "Turn to God. Turn away from SIN!"
Narrator #1: Boys:	*(Hold up the "Boys!" sign)* He followed the Lord! He followed the Lord!
Narrator #2: Girls:	*(Hold up the "Girls!" sign)* Hezekiah was a guy who followed the Lord!

(Repeat the chorus again)

Narrator #1:	He gathered all the teachers at the doors of the CHURCH,
Narrator #2:	And he told everyone to make a careful SEARCH.
Narrator #1:	*(As Hezekiah)* "Find anything and everything that God wouldn't LIKE. Throw it out! That junk's gotta take a HIKE!"
Narrator #1: Boys:	*(Hold up the "Boys!" sign)* He followed the Lord! He followed the Lord!
Narrator #2: Girls:	*(Hold up the "Girls!" sign)* Hezekiah was a guy who followed the Lord!

(Repeat the chorus again)

Narrator #2:	For 16 days they cleaned and they PRAYED,
Narrator #1:	And they threw out the idols that their parents MADE.
Narrator #2:	They turned on the lights and they fixed the DOORS.
Narrator #1:	They wiped the walls and they mopped the FLOORS!
Narrator #1: Boys:	*(Hold up the "Boys!" sign)* He followed the Lord! He followed the Lord!
Narrator #2: Girls:	*(Hold up the "Girls!" sign)* Hezekiah was a guy who followed the Lord!

(Repeat the chorus again)

Narrator #2:	They cleaned the place and made special BREAD,
Narrator #1:	And they told Hezekiah,
Narrator #2:	*(As a helper)* "We've done what you SAID! Everything is ready; now what should we DO?"
Narrator #1:	*(As Hezekiah)* "Commit it to the Lord and commit yourselves, TOO!"
Narrator #1: Boys:	*(Hold up the "Boys!" sign)* He followed the Lord! He followed the Lord!

Wholehearted Hezekiah

Narrator #2:	*(Hold up the "Girls!" sign)*
Girls:	**Hezekiah was a guy who followed the Lord!**

(Repeat the chorus again)

Narrator #1:	**Good job everyone!**
Narrator #2:	**The winner is the . . .** *(Say either "boys" or "girls" whichever group was louder!)*

(ACT 2 – HEZEKIAH GETS SICK OF BEING SICK)

Director:	**Lights! . . . Camera! . . . Action!**
Narrator:	**One day, Isaiah the prophet came to tell Hezekiah some news.**
Isaiah:	**King Hezekiah?**
Hezekiah:	**Yes, Isaiah?**
Isaiah:	**I've got some good news and some bad news.**
Hezekiah:	**Well, give me the good news first.**
Isaiah:	**The good news is that there's not a lot of bad news.**
Hezekiah:	**Oh. What's the bad news?**
Isaiah:	**Well, you know how you're really sick right now?**
Hezekiah:	*(Cough)* **Yeah, so?** *(Cough, cough)*
Isaiah:	**Well, you're not gonna be sick for long—**
Hezekiah:	**That sounds like the good news!** *(Cough, cough)*
Isaiah:	**—because you're gonna be dead.**
Hezekiah:	**Oh. That is bad news. . . .**
Isaiah:	**Told you.**
Narrator:	**And Hezekiah was very sad and cried.**
Hezekiah:	**Waa! Waa!** *(Cough, cough)* **Waa! Waa!** *(Cough, cough)*
Narrator:	**And then he prayed.**
Hezekiah:	*(Praying)* **God! I've followed you with all my heart! Remember that now, please! Save me!** *(Cough, cough)*
Narrator:	**Well, before Isaiah could even leave the palace, God told him to go back and tell Hezekiah some more news.**
Isaiah:	**King Hezekiah?**
Hezekiah:	**Yes, Isaiah?** *(Cough, cough)*
Isaiah:	**I've got some good news and some bad news.**
Hezekiah:	**Oh, no, not this again. . . . Give me the bad news first this time.**
Isaiah:	**The bad news is that there's not a lot of good news.**
Hezekiah:	**Oh. What's the good news?**
Isaiah:	**Well, you know how you're really sick right now?**
Hezekiah:	*(Cough)* **Yeah, so?** *(Cough, cough)*
Isaiah:	**Well, you're not gonna be sick for long.**
Hezekiah:	**Yeah, you told me already . . . I'm gonna be dead. . . .**
Isaiah:	**No, you're not—at least not for awhile! God's gonna heal you! He's gonna give you 15 more years of life!**
Hezekiah:	**Hm . . . how will I know this for sure?**
Isaiah:	**Well, to prove it, God can make the shadow go forward or backward on the sundial. What do you want?**
Hezekiah:	**Hm . . . it always goes forward.** *(Cough, cough)* **Have God make the shadow go backward!**
Isaiah:	**No problemo.**

Wholehearted Hezekiah

Narrator:	And then it happened just like Isaiah had said!
Hezekiah:	Whoa! I'm feeling better already! *(Do some jumping jacks)*
Isaiah:	Here, spread this medicine from fig plants on your sores.
Hezekiah:	Wow! I feel as good as new! You should bottle that stuff. You could make a fortune. . . .
Narrator:	After Hezekiah got better, he wrote a poem of thanks to God.
Hezekiah:	Roses are red. Violets are blue. I'm no longer sick, so I'm thankful to you!
Narrator:	Well, something like that. But he did make a few mistakes.
Hezekiah:	Oops.
Narrator:	After he'd been healed, he became proud.
Hezekiah:	*(Sadly)* Bad news.
Narrator:	But then he humbled himself and God forgave him.
Hezekiah:	*(Happily)* Good news!
Narrator:	When the people in Babylon heard that God had healed him, they sent some men to talk with him. Hezekiah invited them in and showed them all around the palace.
Isaiah:	King Hezekiah?
Hezekiah:	Yes, Isaiah?
Isaiah:	What did those guys want?
Hezekiah:	Oh, well, they were from Babylon.
Isaiah:	Uh-huh . . .
Hezekiah:	And they came 'cause they heard I was sick. . . .
Isaiah:	Uh-huh . . .
Hezekiah:	And I showed 'em around. . . .
Isaiah:	Uh-huh . . . and what did you show 'em, exactly?
Hezekiah:	Um . . . everything . . . I gave 'em the grand tour. . . .
Isaiah:	Guess what?
Hezekiah:	You've got some good news and some bad news?
Isaiah:	How did you ever guess?
Hezekiah:	*(Sigh)* Give me the bad news first. . . .
Isaiah:	God wasn't happy that you did that. He's gonna let them take over this land.
Hezekiah:	Ouch . . . that is bad news. . . . So, what's the good news?
Isaiah:	The good news is that that's all the bad news.
Hezekiah:	Hm . . . well, it sounds like at least there'll be peace while I'm alive, so I guess it's not so bad after all.
Narrator:	And so Hezekiah served the Lord and honored him. He obeyed and loved God. And he followed God with all of his heart.
Isaiah:	And that's the best news of all!
Everyone:	*(Together)* The end!

(Smile, bow, and then take your seat.)

Wholehearted Hezekiah

THE SACK OF SENNACHERIB

BASED ON: 2 Kings 18:17–19:37; Isaiah 36–37; 2 Chronicles 32:1-23

BIG IDEA: When King Sennacherib threatened Jerusalem, God heard the prayers of his people and intervened. God protected the city and sent an angel to demolish the Assyrian army.

BACKGROUND: Hezekiah apparently withheld tax money from the Assyrian overlords (see 2 Kings 18:13-16). Eventually he changed his mind and sent the money; however, King Sennacherib (king of the Assyrians) accepted the money but not the apology. He sent his army commander to besiege Jerusalem.

As a result of the faith and prayers of his people, God spared the city. As a result of the pride of Sennacherib, God decimated his army.

God proved once again that he is sovereign, in control, and more powerful than even the world's most powerful leader.

NEW TESTAMENT CONNECTION: Hezekiah wasn't intimidated by the threats of the pagan king because he relied totally on God. The first thing we can do when bullies try to make us feel bad is to talk to God, trust in him, and then let him be our source of strength. "Finally, be strong in the Lord and in his mighty power" (Ephesians 6:10).

CAST: You'll need 5 children for this QuickSkit: Narrator (girl or boy), Shebna (girl or boy), Commander of the Bad Guys (preferably a boy), Hezekiah (preferably a boy), Isaiah (preferably a boy)

PROPS: None

TOPICS: Bullies, conviction, God's sovereignty, integrity, leadership, obedience, prayer, priorities

TIPS: Position Shebna and Isaiah next to Hezekiah. Place the other readers where you wish onstage. Bring up the stage lights, and then begin when the listeners are quiet.

Director: Lights! . . . Camera! . . . Action!

Narrator: Hezekiah heard that King Sennacherib was planning to attack.

Hezekiah: Quick!

Shebna: Yes, your majesty?

Hezekiah: We need to protect ourselves!

Shebna: But how?

Hezekiah: Hm . . . first, let's make a dam and keep the water away from the fields so if the bad guys surround us they won't have anything to drink.

Shebna: Good idea, your majesty.

Hezekiah: Then rebuild the walls and strengthen the towers!

Shebna: Yes, your majesty!

Hezekiah: Hurry, now! Then gather the people so I can speak to them!

Narrator:	Then Hezekiah encouraged the people.
Hezekiah:	Don't be afraid! God is in control! He'll help us win this battle!
Shebna:	Praise the Lord! He's in control!
Narrator:	Soon, the army commander from King Sennacherib arrived and tried to scare the people in Jerusalem into giving up.
Commander:	*(Acting really tough)* What makes you think you'll be OKAY? We're gonna get you guys TODAY! Your Egyptian friends can't help you NOW! 'Cause your God sent us to wipe you OUT!
Narrator:	Now that wasn't true, of course. The Commander was just trying to make the people doubt Hezekiah and the Lord. Hezekiah's friend, Shebna, who was a leader, was there listening.
Shebna:	Stop talking in the Jewish language! All the people can hear you! Talk to us in another language!
Narrator:	But the Commander just laughed.
Commander:	I want 'em all to hear what I SAY! 'Cause I want everybody to be AFRAID!
Narrator:	Then he yelled out to the people of Jerusalem so they could all hear and understand him:
Commander:	My country is the strongest and the greatest of ALL! We've made every other kingdom FALL! Surrender now, before the wars BEGIN! Your God can't save you! And you'll never WIN!
Narrator:	The people just listened quietly because Hezekiah had told them not to say anything. Then Hezekiah's friends came to tell him what the Commander had said.
Shebna:	King Hezekiah! Their Commander threatened us and made fun of the Lord! What should we do?
Hezekiah:	We'll pray! . . . Isaiah?
Isaiah:	Yes?
Hezekiah:	Pray to the Lord with me!
Isaiah:	OK!
Narrator:	So Isaiah and Hezekiah prayed. And God answered their prayer.
Isaiah:	King Hezekiah?
Hezekiah:	Yes?
Isaiah:	I've got some good news and some bad news.
Hezekiah:	Oh, no.
Isaiah:	It's good news for you and bad news for them.
Hezekiah:	Oh, good.
Isaiah:	God says not to be afraid of 'em. They have insulted both you and the Lord! But God says he will save you and the whole city!
Hezekiah:	Praise the Lord! He's in control!
Narrator:	Meanwhile, God sent another enemy to attack the Assyrian army—
Commander:	Uh-oh.
Narrator:	—and the Commander had to go and fight them. So he sent a letter to Hezekiah,

The Sack of Sennacherib

Commander: We've beaten other gods; we'll beat yours, TOO! You're never gonna win! We're comin' for YOU!

Isaiah: I wouldn't say those things. . . .

Shebna: Their Commander threatened us again . . . and made fun of the Lord again! What should we do?

Hezekiah: Pray, of course!

Narrator: So Hezekiah spread the army commander's letter out, and he prayed to the Lord . . .

Hezekiah: (Praying) O, Lord! You're the only God! Now this king has insulted you! What will you do? He's beaten the other countries who have pretend gods. But they were only stone and wood. You're real! Help us, God, so everyone everywhere will know that you alone are God!

Narrator: And God sent another message to Isaiah.

Isaiah: Here is what the Lord says, "That king has insulted me! When he won wars, I was the one letting him win! But since he yelled at me, now I'm coming after him! . . ."

Narrator: That was good news for Israel.

Isaiah: Hezekiah?

Hezekiah: Yes, Isaiah? Wait, lemme guess . . . good news and bad news?

Isaiah: Actually, just good news this time. That king won't capture this city. God will totally protect us.

Hezekiah: Praise the Lord! He's in control!

Narrator: And that night, God sent a single angel to kill off 185,000 of the bad guys.

Hezekiah: Whoa. That's a lot of bad guys.

Isaiah: That's a lot of dead guys.

Commander: I hope I'm not one of them.

Narrator: You are.

Commander: Oh. Bummer.

Narrator: When they woke up in the morning, there were dead men everywhere . . .

Commander: Uh-oh. Maybe their God is gonna win after all. . . .

Narrator: So the bad guys went back to their city, and God rescued Jerusalem and proved once again that he is in control.

Everyone: (Together) Praise the Lord! He's in control! The end!

(Smile, bow, and then take your seat.)

The Sack of Sennacherib

FUNNY NAMES AND A FIERY FURNACE

BASED ON: Daniel 3

BIG IDEA: When King Nebuchadnezzar ordered everyone to bow and worship his golden statue, three Jewish men refused to obey. God rescued them and revealed his mighty power to the unbelieving king.

BACKGROUND: King Nebuchadnezzar was one of the most powerful rulers in the world. When he ordered everyone in the land to worship his statue, only a handful of people resisted. When they did, they were thrown into the fiery furnace, but God rescued them! They became heroes and witnesses in the land.

NEW TESTAMENT CONNECTION: The boldness and courage of these three men serve as an example for us today: "But in your hearts set apart Christ as Lord. Always be prepared to give an answer to everyone who asks you to give the reason for the hope that you have. But do this with gentleness and respect" (1 Peter 3:15).

CAST: You'll need 6-8 children for this QuickSkit: Narrator (girl or boy), 1-3 Leaders (girls or boys), King Neb (preferably a boy), Shadrach (preferably a boy), Meshach (preferably a boy), Abednego (preferably a boy)

PROPS: Musical instruments, or pots and pans to bang around (optional)

TOPICS: Angels, choices, conviction, courage, faith, following God, God's power, integrity, obedience, prayer, witnessing, worship

TIPS:
- The Leader has a rather goofy part. Choose a child who likes to ham it up as the reader for this part. (You could use up to three people for this part.) If desired, hand out some instruments to volunteer musicians from the audience.
- Make sure that whoever you choose to read the parts of the Narrator and King Neb can actually pronounce the name "Nebuchadnezzar"!
- Position Shadrach, Meshach, and Abednego next to each other on the left side of the stage; the Narrator in the center; and the Leader(s) and King next to each other on the right side of the stage. Bring up the stage lights, and then begin when the listeners are quiet.

Director: **Lights! . . . Camera! . . . Action!**

Narrator: **One day, King Nebuchadnezzar set up a statue 90 feet tall.**

King Neb: *(Excitedly)* **C'mon everybody! Come see my statue!**

Leader: **Okee-dokee, King Nudder-Butter.**

King Neb: **That's Nebuchadnezzar.**

Leader: **Oh, yeah. Right.**

Narrator: **So all the leaders in the land gathered around the statue.**

Leader: **That's a very shiny statue, King Fuzzy-Sweater.**

King Neb:	Thank you. And it's King Nebuchadnezzar.
Leader:	Oh, yeah. Right. Hee, hee, hee, hee.
King Neb:	*(Proudly)* It's golden.
Leader:	Ooh . . .
King Neb:	*(Proudly)* And tall.
Leader:	Aah . . .
King Neb:	And everyone must worship the statue when the music starts.
Leader:	Um . . . what happens if we don't?
King Neb:	You'll be burned alive in a big fiery furnace.
Leader:	Oh. I see. . . .
Narrator:	Then, the music started. *(If you're using musicians, they can clang their instruments at this time)*
Narrator:	And the people bowed. . . . Well, most of the people did.
Leader:	Um, King Never-Eat-Cheddar, three men won't bow.
King Neb:	What? Where are they?! And, um, it's King Nebuchadnezzar, by the way.
Leader:	Oh, yeah. Right. Hee, hee, hee, hee.
King Neb:	Bring them to me!
Three Guys:	*(Together)* Here we are!
King Neb:	What are your names?
Meshach:	Meshach.
Shadrach:	Shadrach.
Abednego:	Abednego.
King Neb:	Well, Mr. Flea-Shack, Backpack, and A-Funny-Bone—
Meshach:	—that's Meshach.

Shadrach:	Shadrach.
Abednego:	And Abednego—
King Neb:	—right. Is it true that you don't serve my gods or bow to worship my statue?!
Shadrach:	Yup.
Meshach:	Yup.
Abednego:	Yup.
King Neb:	Are you ready to bow and worship when the music starts?
Shadrach:	Nope.
Meshach:	Nope.
Abednego:	Nope.
King Neb:	*(Angrily)* Err! Then I'll burn you alive in a big fiery furnace! And what god could save you then?
Three Guys:	*(Together)* O King Nebuchadnezzar—
King Neb:	—Wow, they got it right—
Shadrach:	—Our God can save us. And he will save us.
Meshach:	But even if he chooses not to save us,
Abednego:	We won't ever worship your statue.
King Neb:	It's golden.
Shadrach:	Yes, I see.
King Neb:	And tall.
Meshach:	Right.
King Neb:	And shiny.
Abednego:	Very nice. But we're not gonna worship it.
King Neb:	Err! Alright then! That's it! Tie 'em up and toss 'em in!

Funny Names and a Fiery Furnace

Narrator:	And so, some of the strongest soldiers in King Nob-On-His-Head-There's army—
King Neb:	Um, that's Nebuchadnezzar's army.
Narrator:	Oh, yeah. Right . . . tied up those three men, and tossed 'em into the fiery furnace which was rather like a large barbeque pit.
Shadrach:	Wee!
Meshach:	Wee!
Abednego:	Wee!
King Neb:	Um, didn't we throw three men in there?
Leader:	Yes, King Nibble-Your-Nezzar.
King Neb:	That's King Nebuchadnezzar! Then how come I see four men in there? And how come one of them looks like a god?
Leader:	Um, I dunno. . . .
King Neb:	Hey, Brick-Shack, Shady-Pack and A-Bendy-Bow come on out!
Three Guys:	*(Together)* That's Meshach, Shadrach, and Abednego.
King Neb:	Oh, yeah. Right . . . um, are you okay?
Shadrach:	Yup.
Meshach:	Yup.
Abednego:	Yup.
King Neb:	You're not well done? Burned to a crisp? Or fried alive?
Shadrach:	Nope.
Meshach:	Nope.
Abednego:	Nope.

Narrator:	All the leaders gathered around them. They couldn't believe that the men weren't burned, their hair wasn't singed, and their clothes didn't even smell like smoke.
Leader:	They must have been in the nonsmoking section.
King Neb:	Um, I don't think so. . . . Praise be to their God! These men would rather die than worship any other god than their own.
Shadrach:	Yup.
Meshach:	Yup.
Abednego:	Yup.
King Neb:	From now on, if anyone says anything bad about their God, we'll cut him up into little tiny pieces and then we'll bulldoze his house into the ground! Yeah, that's what we'll do!
Shadrach:	He's rather violent, don't you think?
Meshach:	I should say so.
Abednego:	Me, too.
Shadrach:	Yup.
Meshach:	Yup.
Abednego:	Yup.
Narrator:	Then the king promoted them. And people all over the kingdom heard about the Lord. Because of those three brave men.
Meshach:	Meshach.
Shadrach:	Shadrach.
Abednego:	And Abednego.
Everyone:	*(Together)* The end!

(Smile, bow, and then take your seat.)

Funny Names and a Fiery Furnace

THE GHOSTLY GRAFFITI

BASED ON: Daniel 5

BIG IDEA: God's judgment falls on a wicked king who mocked him and refused to humble himself before the Lord.

BACKGROUND: Daniel is no longer a young man. More than 60 years have passed since he was brought to Babylon. Nebuchadnezzar's grandson, Belshazzar, is now ruling in conjunction with his father Nabonidus. (Some translations call Nebuchadnezzar Belshazzar's "father." The word could also be translated "ancestor." He was actually Belshazzar's grandfather.)

God writes a message on the plaster to get King Belshazzar's attention. Eventually, the king calls in Daniel who delivers a prophetic message of doom to the proud, drunken king.

NEW TESTAMENT CONNECTION: King Nebuchadnezzar and King Belshazzar differed in one important way—only King Nebuchadnezzar humbled himself before God. Humility is one of the essential characteristics of the Christian life. "Therefore, whoever humbles himself like this child is the greatest in the kingdom of heaven" (Matthew 18:4).

CAST: You'll need 6-14 children for this QuickSkit: Narrator (girl or boy), Partygoer (girl or boy), 1-3 Sorcerers (girls or boys), 1-3 Astrologers (girls or boys), 1-3 Wise Men (boys or girls), Queen (girl), King Belshazzar (boy), Daniel (preferably a boy)

PROPS: None

TOPICS: Advice, consequences, ghosts, God's promises, humility, ministry (of the prophets), pride, prophecy fulfillment, rebellion, sin, wisdom

TIPS:
- You have a lot of flexibility with the number of readers for this drama. You could use up to 14 children, or you could use only 6 (by having one person play the parts of all of the Sorcerers, Astrologers, and the Wise Men).
- Make sure that you explain to all the children that the kids playing the part of the Partygoer and King Belshazzar aren't really praying to a false god. They're just saying his lines and pretending to be like the people long ago who didn't love the Lord. Help the audience and the readers understand that there's a difference between acting in a skit and doing something in real life.
- Sometimes the Sorcerers, Astrologers, and Wise Men all speak together. When they do, they are referred to as the Wise Dudes.
- Position the Narrator, the Partygoer, and Daniel next to each other on the right side of the stage; the King and Queen in the center; and the Sorcerers, Astrologers, and Wise Men on the left side of the stage. Bring up the stage lights, and then begin when the listeners are quiet.

Director: **Lights! . . . Camera! . . . Action!**

Narrator: **One day, King Belshazzar gave a big party.**

Belshazzar: **Chips and salsa, anyone?**

Partygoer: **Thank you, O King!**

Narrator: **A thousand people came.**

Belshazzar:	Um . . . I think we're gonna need a few more pizzas. . . .
Narrator:	He drank lots of wine with them. As he did, he felt like showing off.
Belshazzar:	Bring out the gold and silver that Grandpa Neb took from that Jewish temple! . . .
Partygoer:	Here you go, O King!
Belshazzar:	Just take a look at these cups and bowls, everyone!
Partygoer:	Ooh . . . aah . . . ooh . . . aah . . . O King!
Belshazzar:	Impressive, huh?
Partygoer:	Like I said . . . ooh . . . aah . . . ooh . . . aah . . .
Narrator:	Then they poured wine into the golden cups and bowls and started to get drunk! And they started singing praises to their own gods of gold, silver, wood, and stone!
Belshazzar & Partygoer:	*(Together)* Our gods are made of wood and STONE, And gold and steel and StyroFOAM!
Narrator:	Something like that. . . . Suddenly, the fingers of a hand appeared in the air next to the wall!
Belshazzar:	*(Acting really freaked out and scared)* Ah!
Partygoer:	What's wrong, O King? Did you dip your chip in the hot salsa by mistake?
Belshazzar:	*(Stuttering because you're so scared)* H-h-h-hand . . . there's a h-h-h-hand!
Partygoer:	Oh, yeah, I get it! Everybody give the king a HAND! *(Applaud for the king)*
Belshazzar:	No, there's a h-h-h-hand!
Partygoer:	Yeah, I gotta HAND it to you, this is some party, O King!—

Belshazzar:	No! A h-h-h-hand!
Partygoer:	—I'd give it TWO THUMBS UP!
Belshazzar:	H-h-h-hand! . . . H-h-h-hand! . . . H-h-h-hand!
Partygoer:	Yup, this is the best party I've been to all year . . . HANDS down. . . .
Belshazzar:	There is a hand up there! A ghostly hand is writing on the wall!
Partygoer:	*(Acting really freaked out and scared)* Ah!
Narrator:	The king became pale.
Belshazzar:	*(Look pale)*
Narrator:	He got a shocked look on his face.
Belshazzar:	*(Look shocked)*
Narrator:	He got all limp.
Belshazzar:	*(Get all wobbly)*
Narrator:	And his knees began to knock together.
Belshazzar:	*(Knock your knees together)* Sorcerers! Astrologers! Wise men!
Wise Dudes:	*(Together)* Here we are, your majesty!
Belshazzar:	If you can read that writing and explain it to me, I'll give you a promotion, a gold chain, and a purple robe!
Wise Dudes:	*(Together)* Right on!
Narrator:	So the sorcerers tried to read the writing on the wall. . . .
Sorcerers:	Abracadabra-calabra-CADOO! I can't read a word of it, I don't have a CLUE. . . .
Narrator:	Then, the astrologers tried it.

The Ghostly Graffiti

Astrologers:	Starlight, star BRIGHT . . . I wish I may, I wish I MIGHT. Read this writing here TONIGHT . . . I wish I could, but I can't . . . ALRIGHT?!
Narrator:	Finally, the wise men tried to read the writing. . . .
Wise Men:	Mm . . . aha! Mm, hm . . . very interesting. . . .
Belshazzar:	What? Can you read it? Can you explain it to me?
Wise Men:	No, but it IS very interesting. . . .
Belshazzar:	*(Yelling)* Can't anybody help me?!
Wise Dudes:	*(Together)* Sorry, man!
Narrator:	When the king saw that none of his wisest advisors could read the writing, he got even more scared . . .
Belshazzar:	*(Act even more scared than before)*
Narrator:	And his partygoers were totally confused.
Partygoer:	I'm totally confused.
Narrator:	About what?
Partygoer:	I can't find the remote control anywhere. . . .
Narrator:	Um, that's not what confused them. . . . The ghostly writing on the wall did!
Partygoer:	Oh.
Narrator:	Just then, the queen came in.
Belshazzar:	Hey, Queeny baby!
Queen:	Don't call me Queeny baby.
Belshazzar:	OK, Queeny baby!
Queen:	You look really scared!
Belshazzar:	I'm freaked out, baby. I'm totally freaked.
Queen:	Oh. Um, what's with the graffiti?
Belshazzar:	We don't know! That's the problem!
Wise Dudes:	*(Together)* Right on!
Queen:	Oh. Well, back when your Grandpa Neb was king there was a guy he put in charge of all the sorcerers . . .
Sorcerers:	That's us.
Queen:	Astrologers . . .
Astrologers:	That's us.
Queen:	And wise men . . .
Wise Men:	That's us.
Queen:	His name was Daniel.
Daniel:	That's me.
Queen:	God's Spirit was with him. He could interpret dreams, answer riddles, and solve hard problems. Call him and see what he says.
Belshazzar:	Good idea, Queeny baby!
Queen:	Don't call me Queeny baby.
Belshazzar:	OK, Queeny baby!
Narrator:	So they brought Daniel to the party.
Partygoer:	Want something to eat? This salsa is really good. . . .
Wise Dudes:	*(Together)* Right on!
Daniel:	No thanks.
Belshazzar:	Are you Daniel?
Daniel:	Yes, your majesty.
Belshazzar:	Alright, I've heard you're good at interpreting dreams, answering riddles, and solving hard problems.
Daniel:	Well, sometimes, yes.
Wise Dudes:	*(Together)* Right on!

The Ghostly Graffiti

Belshazzar:	Well, if you can read that graffiti over there and explain it to me, I'll give you a promotion, a gold chain, and a purple robe!
Daniel:	Keep your stuff. Give your rewards to someone else. I'm not interested. But I will tell you what the writing says.
Belshazzar:	Cool.
Wise Dudes:	*(Together)* **Right on!**
Daniel:	God made your Grandpa Neb a powerful king. But then, when he bragged, he had to live like a donkey in the fields.
Belshazzar:	I remember. He was really good at giving horsey back rides. . . .
Daniel:	Yeah, well, he eventually humbled himself before God. The problem is, you HAVEN'T, even though you heard all about his story!
Belshazzar:	Um . . . I don't like where this is going. . . .
Daniel:	You brought out the bowls from God's temple and drank wine from them and praised your gods of gold, silver, wood and stone!
Belshazzar:	You didn't like our little Styrofoam rhyme?
Daniel:	No.
Belshazzar:	Oh.
Daniel:	And now God has written this on the wall with his own hand.
Belshazzar:	Oh, boy.
Daniel:	Here's what it says, "Mene, mene, tekel, parsin."
Belshazzar:	Many people tickle Carson? Who's Carson? Why would God write that?
Daniel:	No! Listen, "Mene" means "numbered." It means God has numbered the days of your rule and it's about to end.

Belshazzar:	I don't like the sound of that. . . .
Daniel:	"Tekel" means "weighed." It means you've been weighed on a scale and you're less than you should be.
Belshazzar:	You mean I've lost weight? That's great!
Daniel:	You're not too bright, are you?
Belshazzar:	Nope.
Daniel:	I didn't think so . . . and "Parsin" means "divided." It means God will divide your kingdom between other countries.
Narrator:	When Daniel was done talking, King Belshazzar did as he'd promised. He gave Daniel a promotion, a gold chain, and a purple robe.
Wise Dudes:	*(Together)* **Right on!**
Daniel:	I told you I don't need all this stuff.
Belshazzar:	I know, but take it anyway. A promise is a promise.
Daniel:	Alright. Whatever.
Narrator:	And that very night, King Belshazzar was killed.
Belshazzar:	Ouch!
Narrator:	And a man named Darius became the next king.
Daniel:	God's predictions always come true.
Narrator:	Everything happened just like Daniel had said. And all those people at the party learned an important lesson about pride and about the power of God.
Wise Dudes:	*(Together)* **Right on!**
Everyone:	*(Together)* **The end!**

(Smile, bow, and then take your seat.)

The Ghostly Graffiti

LYIN' IN THE DEN

BASED ON: Daniel 6

BIG IDEA: God rescued Daniel from the lions' den because of his unshakable faith and his life of integrity.

BACKGROUND: Daniel had lived in Babylon for decades and had served as an advisor and leader under several different administrations. Through it all, he showed remarkable integrity and conviction.

In this story, when his political adversaries try to get rid of him, their plan backfires and they end up eliminating themselves from the equation instead.

NEW TESTAMENT CONNECTION: Daniel is a shining example of integrity. He didn't give in and he didn't show off. He simply lived out his faith—simply. We're called to do the same. "In the same way, let your light shine before men, that they may see your good deeds and praise your Father in heaven" (Matthew 5:16).

CAST: You'll need 5 children for this QuickSkit: Narrator (girl or boy), Bad Dude #1 (girl or boy), Bad Dude #2 (girl or boy), King Darius (preferably a boy), Daniel (preferably a boy)

PROPS: None

TOPICS: Angels, conviction, following God, God's power, integrity, leadership, ministry (of the prophets), obedience, sneakiness, success, vengeance, witnessing, worship

TIPS:
- Bad Dude #2 plays a really stupid guy. Have fun with this role!
- Position the Narrator on the right side of the stage, Bad Dude #1 and Bad Dude #2 on the left side, and King Darius and Daniel in the center. Bring up the stage lights, and then begin when the listeners are quiet.

Director: **Lights! . . . Camera! . . . Action!**

Narrator: **King Darius put 120 governors over his kingdom. And he put three men in charge of them all. One of those men was named Daniel.**

Bad Dude #1: **Oh! I hate Daniel!**

Bad Dude #2: *(Stupidly)* **Me, too.**

Bad Dude #1: **I wish he were gone for good.**

Bad Dude #2: **Me, too.**

Bad Dude #1: **Let's try to find something he's done wrong!**

Bad Dude #2: **Me, too! . . . I mean, good idea . . . dude!**

Narrator: **So they watched Daniel closely and checked his work, but they couldn't catch him doing anything wrong at all.**

Bad Dude #1: **Ooh! I wish he'd cheat on his taxes or break the speed limit or shoplift or anything!**

Bad Dude #2: **Me, too . . . um . . . what's shoplifting?**

Bad Dude #1: **It's . . . never mind. Look, Daniel's always praying to his God, right?**

Bad Dude #2:	Uh-huh.
Bad Dude #1:	Well, maybe we can use that against him.
Bad Dude #2:	Good idea, dude! . . . um . . . how are we gonna do that?
Bad Dude #1:	Don't worry . . . I've got a plan.
Bad Dude #2:	Me, too.
Bad Dude #1:	No you don't!
Bad Dude #2:	Oh, yeah. Right. I forgot . . . dude.
Narrator:	So the leaders who didn't like Daniel went before the king with their plan.
Bad Dude #1:	King Darius, may you live forever!
King Darius:	*(Happily)* Well, I hope so!
Bad Dude #2:	Live on, dude!
King Darius:	Thank you!
Bad Dude #1:	We have a great idea! Why don't you make a law that people have to worship you!
King Darius:	Hm . . . sounds good . . .
Bad Dude #1:	And if they don't, you'll feed 'em to some hungry lions!
King Darius:	Sure, why not! They won't live forever.
Bad Dude #1:	No, sir.
King Darius:	Well, then! Let's do it! . . . um, say the thing to me again about me living forever. . . .
Bad Dude #1:	King Darius, may you live forever!
Bad Dude #2:	Live on, dude!
King Darius:	Well, I hope so!
Narrator:	Now, Daniel heard about the new law, but he didn't care. He just went on worshiping God the same as he'd always done.

Bad Dude #1:	Oh, goody! Look at that!
Bad Dude #2:	Yeah, look at that! . . . um . . . look at what?
Bad Dude #1:	Daniel! Look at Daniel! He's praying to his God!
Bad Dude #2:	Look at that! Daniel's praying to his God! . . . Ha, ha, ha . . . um . . . so?
Bad Dude #1:	So we finally got him! Let's go tell the king and he'll throw Daniel into the lion's den!
Bad Dude #2:	Me, too!
Bad Dude #1:	No, not you, too!
Bad Dude #2:	Oh, yeah. Right. I forgot . . . dude.
Bad Dude #1:	Remember that new law you made, your majesty?
King Darius:	Um . . . you didn't say the thing about me living forever. . . .
Bad Dude #1:	*(Sighing)* OK . . . King Darius, may you live forever!
Bad Dude #2:	Live on, dude!
King Darius:	Well, I hope so!
Bad Dude #1:	Now, remember that law?
King Darius:	Yes.
Bad Dude #1:	Well, Daniel broke it! He broke a rule!
Bad Dude #2:	Me, too!
Bad Dude #1:	No, you didn't.
Bad Dude #2:	Oh, yeah. Right. I forgot . . . dude.
Bad Dude #1:	He broke your law! He prayed to his God!
King Darius:	Daniel prayed to his God?!
Bad Dude #1:	Yeah! And now you gotta throw him into the lion's den!
King Darius:	Oh, no!

Bad Dude #2:	Me, too.
Bad Dude #1:	Would you be quiet?
Bad Dude #2:	OK, good idea . . . dude.
Narrator:	The king tried everything he could think of to save Daniel, but it was too late. Once a law in that land was signed, it was final. It couldn't be changed.
King Darius:	Daniel?
Daniel:	Yes, your majesty?
King Darius:	May your God save you!
Daniel:	Well, I hope so.
King Darius:	May you live for tonight!
Daniel:	That, too.
Narrator:	They threw Daniel into the cave where the lions were and rolled a stone in front of the entrance. And all night long the king worried about his friend.
King Darius:	Oh, I can't sleep! Poor Daniel!
Narrator:	That night the king had no food and no dancers or storytellers brought to him.
King Darius:	How could I eat at a time like this?
Narrator:	Early in the morning, he hurried to the cave and had the stone rolled back.
King Darius:	Daniel! Was your God able to save you?
Daniel:	You better believe it . . . um . . . I mean, yeah . . . King Darius, may you live forever!
King Darius:	Well, I hope so!

Daniel:	My God sent his angel and he shut the lions' mouths!
King Darius:	Hooray!
Narrator:	So they pulled Daniel out of the pit.
King Darius:	Now those lions are looking pretty hungry, and I wouldn't want 'em to have to go very long without a good healthy meal. . . .
Bad Dude #2:	Uh-oh.
Bad Dude #1:	Um, we might be in trouble here.
King Darius:	Toss in those guys who were trying to get rid of Daniel!
Bad Dude #1:	I think we're dead meat. . . .
Bad Dude #2:	Me, too. Dude.
King Darius:	Yuck . . . *(Pause)* They didn't live forever.
Daniel:	No they didn't, your majesty.
Narrator:	And the king sent a decree through the land that everyone must respect Daniel's God.
King Darius:	For he's the only one who really will live forever!
Daniel:	You can say that again!
King Darius:	For he's the only one who really will live forever! He saves and rescues and does wonders and miracles!
Daniel:	He saved me!
Narrator:	So after Daniel was saved, God's name was spread throughout the world.
Everyone:	*(Together)* The end!

(Smile, bow, and then take your seat.)

Lyin' in the Den

THE BRAVEST BEAUTY QUEEN*

BASED ON: Esther 1–8

BIG IDEA: Esther's story shows us that God is faithful and works behind the scenes in everyday life to deliver and bless his people.

BACKGROUND: King Xerxes and the Persians had conquered the Israelites and led them into captivity. In his third year of ruling from the city of Susa, King Xerxes banished his queen. After a nationwide search, he chose a Jewish girl named Esther to be the new queen. This story retells what happened and how God used her courage to protect Jews throughout the empire.

NEW TESTAMENT CONNECTION: Esther placed her life in God's hands when she went before King Xerxes. Paul had the same kind of faith in God: "I eagerly expect and hope that I will in no way be ashamed, but will have sufficient courage so that now as always Christ will be exalted in my body, whether by life or by death" (Philippians 1:20). And we pray the same thing, too.

CAST: You'll need 5 children for this QuickSkit: Narrator (girl or boy), Haman (preferably a boy), Mordecai (preferably a boy), King Xerxes (preferably a boy), Esther (girl)

PROPS: None

TOPICS: Advice, bullies, choices, conviction, courage, family relationships, following God, God's sovereignty, hope, integrity, leadership, planning, prejudice, resentment, success, wisdom

TIPS: Position the Narrator on the right side of the stage, Haman and Mordecai on the left side, and King Xerxes and Esther in the center. Bring up the stage lights, and then begin when the listeners are quiet.

*An earlier version of this script first appeared in *The Creative Storytelling Guide for Children's Ministry* (Standard Publishing, 2002, pages 74, 75). Used by permission.

Director: Lights! . . . Camera! . . . Action!

Narrator: One day long ago, there was a King named King Xerxes.

King Xerxes: Gesundheit.

Narrator: I wasn't sneezing, I was telling them your name.

King Xerxes: Oh, right.

Narrator: Well, one day, he kicked his wife out of the palace because she wouldn't do what he asked her to do.

King Xerxes: Serves her right. That'll teach her!

Narrator: But then, he got really lonely.

King Xerxes: That'll teach me! . . . What am I gonna do? . . . I know! I'll search for a beautiful new queen. Why should I be lonely! After all, I am King Xerxes!

Narrator: Gesundheit.

King Xerxes: Thank you.

Narrator:	So he decided to throw the first beauty pageant ever. His advisors searched throughout the land until they came to a place where there lived a Jewish man named Mordecai.
Mordecai:	That's me!
Narrator:	And his beautiful young cousin, Esther.
Esther:	That's me.
Mordecai:	Esther, you know that since your parents died I've raised you as my own daughter and I've always done what's best for you.
Esther:	Yes, Mordecai. Why are you saying this? What's wrong?
Mordecai:	These men are searching for a new queen for King Xerxes.
King Xerxes:	Gesundheit.
Mordecai:	Who said that?
King Xerxes:	Never mind.
Mordecai:	Anyway, they may try to take you away. If they do, don't tell anyone you're a Jewish girl.
Esther:	But why not, Mordecai?
Mordecai:	Trust me, Esther. There are people out there who don't like Jews.
Esther:	OK, I promise. I'll do as you say.
Narrator:	The advisors DID notice Esther and they DID take her back to the king. And when he saw her, his heart began to flutter.
King Xerxes:	Esther wins the contest! She shall be my new queen!
Narrator:	He placed a crown on Esther's head and threw a big party to celebrate. . . . Now one of the highest officials in the government, a man named Haman, was there.

Haman:	So the king has a new queen. I'm just glad she's not a Jew. I hate 'em all! Especially that guy Mordecai! He never bows before me.
Mordecai:	I never worship people, Haman. I'll never worship you.
Narrator:	Then, one day, Haman had an idea.
Haman:	I know what I'll do. I'll tell the king that all Jews are bad and should be killed! Then I can get rid of Mordecai and all of his people at the same time!
Narrator:	Well, Haman tricked the king into making a law that all the Jews should be killed. And when Mordecai found out, he was very troubled and sad.
Mordecai:	What will we do? Unless something happens, we'll all be goners! . . . I know, I'll send a note to Queen Esther and ask for her help. . . .
Esther:	Hm . . . a letter from Mordecai . . . (Pretending to read a letter) Dear Esther, we're all in danger. Perhaps you've been placed in the palace at this time to help us. Will you ask the king to save us? Love, Mordecai.
Narrator:	Now, you remember how the King treated queens who didn't please him—
Esther:	What shall I do?
Narrator:	Talking to the king without being invited was dangerous—it meant death for anyone who would try it!
Esther:	If the king isn't happy with me, he'll have me killed! But if I don't say something, my family will die.
Narrator:	Finally, Esther agreed to help her people. She went into the throne room and bowed low to the ground. She knew she might not walk out of there alive.
Esther:	O King, have mercy on me!
King Xerxes:	Arise, my queen! What do you want? Don't be afraid. I won't hurt you!

The Bravest Beauty Queen

Esther:	Then come to a special party. I'll ask you a favor then.
King Xerxes:	Splendid! I'll see you there, my dear!
Esther:	And Haman is invited, too.
Haman:	Oh, goody, goody. A party!
Narrator:	Meanwhile, Haman was preparing to have Mordecai hanged. He had a long rope brought in, and ordered his helpers to build a place to hang Mordecai.
Haman:	He'll never bother me again! *(Evil laughter)*
Narrator:	The first party went well and then, a few days later, Esther invited the king and Haman to a second party. It was finally time to ask for the king's help.
Haman:	Oh, goody, goody! Another party! And by the end of the day Mordecai will be hanged. This is gonna be a day to remember!
King Xerxes:	Esther, thank you for this party. Now I think you mentioned there was something important you wanted to ask me. What is it?
Esther:	Save me, O King! Save me and my people from the man who wants to destroy us all!
King Xerxes:	But who? Who would dare to harm my queen?
Esther:	*(Point to Haman)* He would!
King Xerxes:	What?
Haman:	Uh-oh.
Esther:	Our enemy is Haman!
Haman:	This might not be good.
Narrator:	About then, one of the guards said that the place to hang Mordecai was ready.

King Xerxes:	What? But Mordecai is a hero! He warned me when people were planning to kill me! He saved my life! You would kill my queen and the man who saved me?!
Haman:	Uh-oh. This is not going according to plan.
King Xerxes:	Guards! Take him away! You know what to do with him!
Haman:	Um . . . help?
Narrator:	That day, Haman was hanged and the king did what he could to protect the Jews from those who wanted to harm them.
King Xerxes:	Mordecai!
Mordecai:	Yes, your majesty?
King Xerxes:	Tell your people to protect themselves. I don't want any Jews harmed!
Mordecai:	Yes, your majesty!
King Xerxes:	And it seems that with Haman's departure we have a job opening. Would you be interested in being my chief advisor?
Mordecai:	I would be honored, your majesty!
Esther:	Oh, thank you, King Xerxes! You've saved my people.
King Xerxes:	No, Esther. YOU have saved your people.
Narrator:	And ever since that day, Jews around the world have celebrated parties of their own in honor of Esther and the time she helped rescue them from Haman's evil plan by talking to King Gesundheit—
King Xerxes:	Xerxes!
Narrator:	Oh, yeah.
Everyone:	*(Together)* The end!

(Smile, bow, and then take your seat.)

The Bravest Beauty Queen

Scripture Verse Index

* Appears in *30 New Testament QuickSkits for Kids*

Topical Index

Miracles (of the disciples)
His Power, Not Ours!*
Simon the Sorcerer*
The Man Who Wasn't Dead*
The Riot in Ephesus*
Shipwrecked!*

Miracles (of Jesus)
see Jesus' Miracles*

New Life
He Is Alive!*
Yo! Now I See!*
Demon, Demon, Go Away!*
The Return of Lazarus*
He Saw the Light*
Eve: The Apple of Adam's Eye

Obedience
The Garden of Gethsemane*
His Power, Not Ours!*
Happy Trails to You!*
The Man Who Wasn't Dead*
Thou Shalt Not Bite!
Noah and the Zoo Cruise
God Tests Abraham's Faith
The Cow and the Commandments
Balaam and the Talking Donkey
The Attack of the Marching Band
The Voice in the Night
Joash Restores the Temple
Jonah and the Basking Shark
Wholehearted Hezekiah
The Sack of Sennacherib
Funny Names and a Fiery Furnace
Lyin' in the Den

Palm Sunday
Jesus Christ Is Comin' to Town!*

Passover
Toejam Man*
The Garden of Gethsemane*

Patience
Water Into Wine*
When Sarah Delivered God's Punch
  Line
Naomi's New Family

Paul
He Saw the Light*
Praying by the River*
The Man Who Wasn't Dead*
The Riot in Ephesus*
Shipwrecked!*

Pentecost
Goodness, Gracious, Great Tongues of
  Fire!*

Perseverance
The Man Who Wasn't Dead*
Joseph's Journey from the Pit to the
  Palace

Peter
Toejam Man*
The Garden of Gethsemane*
He Is Alive!*
The Transfiguration*
Up, Up and Away!*
Goodness, Gracious, Great Tongues of
  Fire!*
His Power, Not Ours!*
Liar, Liar... Die-er, Die-er*

Pharisees
The Miracle No One Noticed*
Yo! Now I See!*
His Power, Not Ours!*
The Man Who Wasn't Dead*

Planning
Joseph's Journey from the Pit to the
  Palace
Ehud: The Left-handed Assassin
The Bravest Beauty Queen

Prayer
The Garden of Gethsemane*
Demon, Demon, Go Away!*
The Longest Day
Solomon's Radical Wisdom
Showdown on Carmel Mountain
Wholehearted Hezekiah
The Sack of Sennacherib
Funny Names and a Fiery Furnace

Prejudice
Jonah and the Basking Shark
The Bravest Beauty Queen

Pride
Babbling at Babel
Wholehearted Hezekiah
The Ghostly Graffiti

Priorities
What It Takes to Follow Jesus*
Wonder Bread*
The Miracle No One Noticed*
Liar, Liar... Die-er, Die-er*
Simon the Sorcerer*
Wholehearted Hezekiah
The Sack of Sennacherib

Prophecy Fulfillment
The Birth of King Jesus*
Jesus Christ Is Comin' to Town!*
The Death of Jesus*
He Is Alive!*
The Road to Emmaus*
The Transfiguration*
Goodness, Gracious, Great Tongues of
  Fire!*
When Sarah Delivered God's Punch
  Line
The Siege of Samaria
The Ghostly Graffiti

Purpose
The Garden of Gethsemane*
The Death of Jesus*

Water Into Wine*
Wonder Bread*
The Return of Lazarus*

Rebellion
Thou Shalt Not Bite!
Babbling at Babel
The Cow and the Commandments
Jonah and the Basking Shark
The Ghostly Graffiti

Repentance
Goodness, Gracious, Great Tongues of
  Fire!*
Simon the Sorcerer*
Happy Trails to You!*
He Saw the Light*
Wholehearted Hezekiah

Resentment
The Miracle No One Noticed*
Joseph's Journey from the Pit to the
  Palace
The Bravest Beauty Queen

Second Chances
He Is Alive!*
The Miracle No One Noticed*
Yo! Now I See!*
He Saw the Light*
Thou Shalt Not Bite!
Noah and the Zoo Cruise
The Cow and the Commandments
Naomi's New Family
Jonah and the Basking Shark

Service
Toejam Man*

Sin
Liar, Liar... Die-er, Die-er*
Simon the Sorcerer*
Thou Shalt Not Bite!
Noah and the Zoo Cruise
The Cow and the Commandments
The Ghostly Graffiti

Sneakiness
Ehud: The Left-handed Assassin
Lyin' in the Den

Stubbornness
What It Takes to Follow Jesus*
Yo! Now I See!*
The Riot in Ephesus*
Balaam and the Talking Donkey
Jonathan and David: Friends for Life
The Kingdom Is Torn in Two
Jonah and the Basking Shark

Success
Joseph's Journey from the Pit to the
  Palace
The Longest Day
Ehud: The Left-handed Assassin
Cliffhanger!
The Day the Bully Went Down
David's Mighty Men

Solomon's Radical Wisdom
Showdown on Carmel Mountain
Lyin' in the Den
The Bravest Beauty Queen

Suffering
The Death of Jesus*
Healed by Faith*
Demon, Demon, Go Away!*
Naomi's New Family
The Siege of Samaria

Talking Animals
Thou Shalt Not Bite!
Balaam and the Talking Donkey

Temptation
Thou Shalt Not Bite!

Transfiguration, the
The Transfiguration*

Vengeance
Lyin' in the Den

Wedding Cake
Water Into Wine*

Wisdom
The Arrival of the Wise Guys*
Joseph's Journey from the Pit to the
  Palace
Solomon's Radical Wisdom
The Ghostly Graffiti
The Bravest Beauty Queen

Witnessing
Up, Up and Away!*
Goodness, Gracious, Great Tongues of
  Fire!*
His Power, Not Ours!*
Simon the Sorcerer*
Happy Trails to You!*
Praying by the River*
The Man Who Wasn't Dead
Shipwrecked!*
Jonah and the Basking Shark
Funny Names and a Fiery Furnace
Lyin' in the Den

Worship
The Arrival of the Wise Guys*
Jesus Christ Is Comin' to Town!*
He Saw the Light*
The Cow and the Commandments
Showdown on Carmel Mountain
Joash Restores the Temple
Wholehearted Hezekiah
Funny Names and a Fiery Furnace
Lyin' in the Den

Index